PRAYING THE PSALMS

WITH BEADS

PRAYING THE PSALMS WITH BEADS

A Book of Daily Prayers

Nan Lewis Doerr

WILLIAM B. EERDMANS PUBLISHING COMPANY

GRAND RAPIDS, MICHIGAN

Wm. B. Eerdmans Publishing Co.
4035 Park East Court SE, Grand Rapids, Michigan 49546
www.eerdmans.com

26 25 24 23 22 21 20   1 2 3 4 5 6 7

ISBN 978-0-8028-7833-5

Library of Congress Cataloging-in-Publication Data

Names: Doerr, Nan Lewis, author.
Title: Praying the Psalms with beads : a book of daily prayers / Nan
    Lewis Doerr.
Description: Grand Rapids, Michigan : William B. Eerdmans Pub-
    lishing Company, 2020. | Summary: "182 daily prayers based on
    the psalms, intended for use with Anglican prayer beads"—Pro-
    vided by publisher.
Identifiers: LCCN 2020006450 | ISBN 9780802878335 (paperback)
Subjects: LCSH: Bible. Psalms—Devotional use. | Church year—
    Prayers and devotions. | Anglican Communion—Prayers and
    devotions. | Beads—Religious aspects—Anglican Communion.
Classification: LCC BS1430.54 .D64 2020 | DDC 242/.5—dc23
LC record available at https://lccn.loc.gov/2020006450

Contents

Acknowledgments and Thanksgivings

A project like this is never done in isolation. My love and thanks go out to all my friends and associates who have encouraged me along the way and helped to make this book possible:

To Kati Garner who was the original inspiration for this book through a comment she made one night at our Cursillo Reunion Group.

To Vincent William Uher III for his diligence and willingness to check the psalms for theological soundness. To my Delta Zeta sorority sister, Barbara Cloud, for diligently pray-testing the psalms and giving me valuable feedback. To my friend Johneta Turner for her help in writing the introduction, and Charli Merchant for her help in proofreading.

To my husband, Sam, who has put up with late lunches and the dining room table being cluttered with Bibles and commentaries. To our son, Andy, and daughter, Cyndy, for their ongoing support during this process. To my daughter-in-law, Lea Colclasure, for listening to all my rantings and detailed explanations about the process I used for creating this set of prayers.

To my friends the Rev. Beth Noland and Leah Elliott MacKay for their ongoing encouragement and support.

To my mentor, Virginia Stem Owens, for recognizing a talent in me that I couldn't see in myself and encouraging me to pursue it.

And finally, to my great friend, Fleetwood Range, who has been a spiritual presence and guide in my life with Christ.

Introduction

My Encounter with Prayer Beads

During a retreat my senior year in seminary, I discovered the Anglican prayer beads and made my first set of beads. Somehow, that making of beads and praying with them resonated with me in a new way. As I went out to my first placement as campus missioner at Sam Houston State University and assistant at St. Stephen's Episcopal Church, I began to develop prayers to use with the beads. I taught my students at the university and the Daughters of the King at St. Stephen's to make prayer beads and to pray with them on a regular basis. My first book, *Praying with Beads*, written with Virginia Stem Owens, grew out of the prayers I developed there.

The focus of my first book was the Episcopal Lectionary, arranging prayers and Scripture verses to focus on the weekly readings of the Christian year. Each week I could meditate on a small portion of the lessons through using the Anglican prayer beads.

That was my primary focus until January 1, 2019. After reading the lessons for the holy name of Jesus, I felt led to arrange the psalm of the day, Psalm 8, to be used with the prayer beads, and I posted it to my blog, Myprayingwithbeads.blogspot.com.

Several weeks before Lent, I became aware that God was calling me to a new use of the prayer beads: to arrange more psalms to be prayed with beads. I started by creating a booklet of psalms that are used specifically during Lent. By the time Lent ended, I knew God was calling me to arrange the entire psalter for use with prayer beads. This book is the result of following that call.

Why Pray with Beads?

In the introduction to my first book, my coauthor, Virginia Stem Owens, talks about the history of beads and the reasons for using beads as a tool to facilitate praying. She also talks about picking up the ancient practice of counting your prayers.

For me, like so many others, I find that in our busy world it is often hard to slow down enough to focus on praying. And when I sit down to pray, I start off well, but soon my mind will wander off in ten different directions, and I want to jump up to do one thing or another. But the simple act of holding the beads in my hands and working my way through them by touch satisfies my body's need for movement and allows my mind to remain focused on what I am praying. It also reminds me that God is as close to me as the beads I hold in my hand.

Some Background on the Book of Psalms

The book of Psalms is a collection of songs and prayers that were written over a period of about six hundred years. The current book of Psalms is a collection of favorite psalms that have survived centuries of change. Jews call the Psalter "The Book of Praises." The Psalms have been recited, prayed, set to music, and sung by both Jews and Christians as part of their corporate worship, with themes of national or communal interest, and as part of their personal spiritual journey.

There are many types of psalm: laments, songs of Zion, songs of thanksgiving, and songs of praise. There are psalms of confidence, wisdom, and history; there are royalty and enthronement psalms. Other types include messianic psalms that look forward to the coming messiah, psalms of ascents when going up to worship, acrostic psalms that begin with consecutive letters of the Hebrew alphabet, and imprecatory psalms that call for judgment and retribution.

Why Pray the Psalms?

In his introduction to the book of Psalms in *The Life with God Bible*, Richard J. Foster asserts: "Christian writers throughout history have insisted that the only way we can come to understand the psalms is by praying them and using them in ways that allow them to shape us." Like the rest of the Bible, they have something profound to say to us even now. There is much to be learned about how to pray from studying and praying the psalms, and they provide us with a pattern for our own prayers.

The one element that stands out most vividly in the book of Psalms is the honest human emotion that is expressed throughout this collection of songs, written by a variety of authors. Each psalmist pours out his heart and soul to fill the psalm with love, or fear, or excitement, or regret, or confidence, or confusion, or hope. Each tells the story like it is. They recount the details, admit their frustrations, and share their joys. They also ask for God's help, salvation, forgiveness, and even occasionally retribution against the injustices that have been done. These are the unfiltered prayers of faith-filled believers.

In reading the works of Desmond Tutu (*The Book of Forgiving*, 2015) and Brené Brown (*Rising Strong*, 2017), I have discovered the value of being able to tell the unfiltered story as one understands it. The first step to acceptance, understanding, healing, and reconciliation is to be honest about what we are feeling. Then we can work our way through our initial emotions to begin to find balance on the other side.

This is good news for us, because it gives us a pattern for our own prayers. It helps us understand the kind of honesty we can share with God. The thing that God wants most from us is a relationship where we can be honest about our own feelings and confident enough in God's grace to share not only our joy but also our fears, hopes, frustrations, dreams—even our sins. God knows them all anyway, but it is in the telling that we begin to heal and understand and see a path out of darkness into true relationship.

About the Prayers

To do this I have chosen to arrange the entire psalter into prayers for use with the beads. Because some psalms are quite long, they have been broken into multiple prayers. This allows the psalms to be prayed in bite-sized portions that are easy to manage. The 150 psalms have become 182 prayers that can each be prayed in under five minutes. I envision a person being able to pray the entire psalter twice in one year using these prayers, one each day.

The psalms in this book are not any particular translation. I began with the translation found in *The Book of Common Prayer*, 1979, which is in the public domain. I consulted several other translations during the writing, along with Hebrew dictionaries, in order to make the most sense of the text. The psalms have been adapted to facilitate their use with the prayer beads. One of these adaptations concerns "Selah," a term that appears in many psalms and may indicate a pause in the lyrics for an instrumental interlude. For the purpose of prayer, I will omit those references.

My intent was to maintain the integrity of each psalm while providing the richest experience possible of using the psalms as personal prayer when focused through the Anglican or Christian prayer beads.

The body or narrative of each psalm is carried primarily in the "invitatory" bead and the "cruciform" beads. The cross will often carry the beginning and end of the narrative, but occasionally will serve as a focus or overview for the psalm. The "weeks" beads will sometimes continue the narrative, but other times they will either respond to the narrative or comment on it.

As I worked my way through the psalms, I found that some of the psalms really needed context to understand what was going on. I think too many of us, myself included, tend to read through a psalm, occasionally picking up on a clue here and there, but not really understanding what is happening.

Just as it helps us understand a book better to know if it is a novel, or a biography, or a do-it-yourself book, it may help us to understand something about the psalm we are reading to know about its type or context, so I have included this information at the start of each psalm. The Bible attributes some psalms to particular authors, and in these cases I note the author at the beginning of the text. Many scholars agree that, in some cases, a psalm may have been written by someone else about the person named or as a tribute to that person. I also add notes about context or interesting elements.

My hope is that you find understanding, comfort, and healing as you pray your way through the book of Psalms. I sincerely hope that you find value and depth of experience with God through using these prayers.

Anglican Prayer Beads

The Anglican Rosary© was developed by the Rev. Lynn Bauman and a group of Episcopalians as an aid to contemplative prayer. They contain a San Damiano cross and thirty-three beads, five large beads and twenty-eight smaller beads. Thirty-two of the beads form a circle, with four of the large beads each separated by seven smaller beads. The four larger beads form a cross when the beads are held out and are therefore called "cruciform" beads. The four groups of smaller beads are called "weeks," reminding us of the days of the week and the days of creation. A week, consisting of seven days, is significant because seven is considered the number of completeness by Christians. All thirty-three beads remind us of the number of years of Jesus's life, and the cross reminds us how Jesus died for us. The one larger bead outside the circle is called the "invitatory" bead, for it invites us into the circle of prayer.

The Prayer Beads Pattern

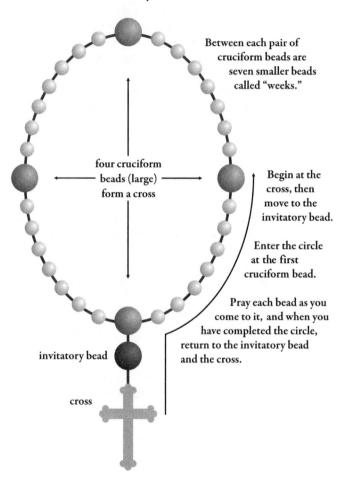

Between each pair of cruciform beads are seven smaller beads called "weeks."

four cruciform beads (large) form a cross

Begin at the cross, then move to the invitatory bead.

Enter the circle at the first cruciform bead.

Pray each bead as you come to it, and when you have completed the circle, return to the invitatory bead and the cross.

invitatory bead

cross

✝   represents the cross.
✿   represents the invitatory bead.
❖   represents the four cruciform beads.
●   represents the seven weeks beads.

How to Pray the Anglican Beads Using This Book

See diagram.

- **✝** Always begin at the cross. Holding it in your hand, pray the prayer shown at the first **✝**.

- **✪** Move to the large invitatory bead nearest the cross. Hold it in your hand and pray this prayer.

  - **❖¹** Move now to the next large bead. This is the first of four cruciform beads in the circle. Hold it in your hand and pray the prayer shown.

  - **●** Move now to the seven weeks beads following the first cruciform bead. Pray this verse seven times, once on each bead.

  - **❖²** Move to the next cruciform bead and pray this prayer.

  - **●** Pray this prayer on the next seven beads.

  - **❖³** and **❖⁴** Continue in the same fashion as above.

  - **❖** When you reach the starting cruciform bead, pray this prayer.

- **✪** Go back out to the invitatory bead and read this prayer.

- **✝** Now finish by using the final prayer at the cross.

Month One

• • • • •

Psalms 1–29

Psalm 1

Psalm 1 is a wisdom psalm by an unknown author. For many wisdom psalms, the author is unnamed. This psalm contrasts those who are righteous with sinners, introducing a concept that will be seen throughout the psalms.

✝ Happy are all who delight in the law of the LORD.

☉ Blessed are those who do not follow the advice of the wicked, or walk in the way of sinners, or sit in the seat of the scornful.

❖¹ Their delight is in the law of the LORD, and on God's law they will meditate day and night.

● Blessed are those who trust in the LORD.

❖² They are like trees planted by streams of water, bearing fruit in due season, with leaves that do not wither.

● They will prosper in everything they undertake.

❖³ It is not so with the wicked; they are like chaff which the wind blows away.

● The wicked will be blown away like chaff.

❖⁴ The wicked will not stand upright when judgment comes, nor will the sinner remain in the council of the righteous.

● Blessed are those who trust in the LORD.

❖ For the LORD watches over the righteous, but the way of the wicked will perish.

☉ Blessed are those who do not follow the advice of the wicked, or walk in the way of sinners, or sit in the seat of the scornful.

✝ Happy are all who delight in the law of the LORD.

Psalm 2

This royal psalm has messianic overtones, seen in the use of the term "Anointed." Again the author is unknown.

✝ Happy are those who take refuge in the LORD our God.

✿ Why are the nations in an uproar? Why do they waste their time with futile plans? The kings of the earth rise up in revolt, and the rulers plot against the LORD's Anointed.

❖¹ "Let us break the chains and free ourselves from slavery to God," they say. The LORD in heaven is amused by their presumption.

● God expressed displeasure, terrifying them with great fury.

❖² This is the decree of the LORD: "I have set my king upon my holy hill, Zion." And God said,

● "You are my son; today have I become your Father.

❖³ Ask of me and I will give you the nations for your inheritance and the whole earth for your possession.

● They are yours to crush with an iron rod or shatter like pottery."

❖⁴ Rulers of the nations, be wise and show discernment. Be warned, judges of the earth.

● Serve the LORD with reverence and rejoice with trembling.

❖ Submit to God's Son and honor him, or his anger may be kindled and you would perish.

✿ "Ask of me and I will give you the nations for your inheritance and the whole earth for your possession."

✝ Happy are all who take refuge in the LORD.

Psalm 3

This is a psalm of confidence by David when he fled from Absalom, his son.

✝ Deliverance belongs to the LORD. Let your blessing be upon all your people.

✿ O LORD, how many are my foes! They rise up all around me.

❖ [1] How many are saying of me that there will be no help for me from my God!

● Yet, still I raise my voice to cry out to the LORD.

❖ [2] You, O LORD, are my shield and my glory. You are the one who lifts up my head.

● O God, you answer me from your holy hill.

❖ [3] I lie down and go to sleep; I wake again, because the LORD sustains me.

● O God, answer me when I cry out to you.

❖ [4] I do not fear the multitude of people who set themselves against me.

● Rise up, O LORD, and set me free.

❖ Surely my God will strike my enemies and break the teeth of the wicked.

✿ Deliverance belongs to the LORD. Let your blessing be upon all your people.

✝ Let your blessing, O LORD, be upon all your people.

Psalm 4

This is a psalm of confidence by David, an evening psalm reflecting on the events of the day.

✝ Answer me when I call, O righteous God.

☉ Answer me when I call, O God, defender of my cause. You set me free when I am hard-pressed. Have mercy on me and hear my prayer.

❖¹ "You mortals, how long will you dishonor my glory; how long will you worship dumb idols and run after false gods?" Hear me when I call.

● For you, O Lord, work wonders for your faithful people.

❖² Tremble, then, and do not sin; speak to your heart in silence upon your bed.

● Offer the appointed sacrifices and put your trust in the Lord.

❖³ Many are saying, "Oh, that we might see better times!" Lift up the light of your countenance upon us, O Lord.

● You, Lord, have put gladness in my heart.

❖⁴ You have put gladness in my heart, more than when grain and wine and oil increase.

● I lie down in peace; at once I fall asleep.

❖ I lie down in peace; at once I fall asleep, for only you, Lord, make me dwell in safety.

☉ Answer me when I call, O God, defender of my cause. You set me free when I am hard-pressed. Have mercy on me and hear my prayer.

✝ You, O Lord, have put gladness in my heart.

Psalm 5

Psalm 5 is an individual lament of David. It is a morning prayer in which David seeks insight against his enemies.

✝ Give ear to my words, O LORD my God; consider the meditation of my heart.

☉ Listen to my cry for help, my King and my God, as I make my prayer to you.

❖¹ In the morning, LORD, you hear my voice; then I will make my request and wait for you. O God, you take no pleasure in wickedness, and evil cannot dwell with you.

● Early in the morning, LORD, my cry comes to you.

❖² The proud cannot stand in your sight. You hate all who do evil, the bloodthirsty and deceitful; and you destroy those who speak lies.

● Through your abundant and steadfast love, I dare to enter your house.

❖³ Lead me, O LORD, in your righteousness, past those who lie in wait for me; make your way straight before me.

● I will bow down toward your holy temple in awe of you.

❖⁴ For there is no truth in their mouth, only destruction in their heart and flattery on their lips. All who take refuge in you will be glad.

● Those who take refuge in you will sing out their joy forever.

❖ Declare them guilty, O God, those who scheme against you. Cast them out because of their sin, for they have rebelled against you.

☉ Let all who take refuge in you be glad and sing out their joy forever. Shelter them, so that all who love your name may exult in you.

✝ For you, O LORD, will bless the righteous; you surround them with your shield of love.

Psalm 6

This individual lament of David is a prayer for recovery from illness. It is a penitential psalm in which David does not plead his innocence but asks only for God's grace. This psalm gives an example of the very personal way the psalmist views and relates to God.

✝ O LORD, deliver me; come and save me for your mercy's sake.

☉ LORD, do not rebuke me in your anger nor punish me in your wrath.

❖¹ Have pity on me, LORD, for I am weak; heal me, LORD, for my bones are in agony.

● O LORD, save me; deliver me in your steadfast love.

❖² My spirit shakes with terror. How long, O LORD, will this continue? In death no one remembers you; and who will give you thanks from the grave?

● Turn, O LORD, and deliver me; save me for your mercy's sake.

❖³ I grow weary of groaning; every night I drench my bed and flood my couch with tears.

● O LORD, hear my supplication and receive my prayer.

❖⁴ My eyes are wasted with grief and worn away because of all my enemies.

● The LORD has heard my supplication; the LORD accepts my prayer.

❖ Depart from me, all evildoers, for the LORD has heard the sound of my weeping.

☉ All my enemies shall be confounded and quake with fear; they shall turn back and suddenly be put to shame.

✝ The LORD has heard my supplication; the LORD accepts my prayer.

Psalm 7

David sang this *shiggaion* to the LORD as an individual lament concerning a friend who betrayed him. A *shiggaion* is a song probably of trouble or comfort.

✝ O LORD, my God, in you I take refuge. Save me and deliver me from all my enemies,

☉ Lest they tear me apart like a lion and haul me away where none can deliver me.

❖¹ O LORD, if I have done evil against one who is my friend or without cause, then let my enemy pursue and catch me and trample my life into the ground. Stand up in your wrath,

● O LORD, rise up against the fury of my enemies.

❖² Awake, O God, decree justice, let the assembly gather round you. Be seated on your throne and judge the nations.

● O LORD, judge me according to my righteousness and my innocence.

❖³ Almighty God, you search the mind and heart of all. Bring an end to the violence of the wicked and establish the righteous.

● God is my shield, who saves the true of heart.

❖⁴ If they do not repent, God will whet the sword and bend the bow to make it ready.

● God is a righteous judge who sits in judgment every day.

❖ God has prepared weapons of death and makes arrows that are shafts of fire.

☉ Look at those whose labor of evil gives birth to a lie. They dig a deep pit and fall in it. Their evil intent returns to trap them.

✝ O LORD, you are the Righteous One. I will sing praise to your holy name.

Psalm 8

Divine majesty and human dignity are seen in this psalm of praise and thanksgiving by David. Here we are reminded that God created the world out of covenant love.

✝ O LORD our Governor, how exalted is your name in all the world!

✪ Out of the mouths of infants and children your majesty is praised above the heavens.

❖¹ You have set up a stronghold against your adversaries, to quell the enemy and the avenger.

● O LORD our God, how majestic is your name in all the earth!

❖² When I consider your heavens, the work of your fingers, the moon and the stars you have set in their courses,

● Who are we that you should be mindful of us and seek us out?

❖³ You have made us but a little lower than the angels; you adorn us with glory and honor.

● Adonai, our LORD, how glorious is your name throughout the earth!

❖⁴ You give us mastery over the works of your hands; you put all things under our feet.

● You seek us out, O LORD, and clothe us with authority.

❖ Even the wild beasts of the field, the sheep, and the oxen you place under our authority.

✪ The birds of the air, the fish of the sea, and whatever walks in the path of the sea you place under our authority.

✝ O LORD our Governor, how exalted is your name in all the world!

Psalm 9

This is David's song of thanksgiving, possibly to celebrate his victory over Goliath. It is an acrostic poem with stanzas beginning with successive letters of the first half of the Hebrew alphabet. It pairs with Psalm 10, which contains the second half of the alphabet.

✝ I will be glad and sing your praise, O Lord. Let my enemies be driven back, to stumble and perish in your presence.

✪ You, Lord, have maintained my just cause; you sit upon your throne as a righteous judge.

❖¹ You have rebuked the ungodly, destroyed the wicked, and blotted out their name. The enemy is finished, and their cities are ruined, and the memory of them has vanished.

● The Lord is enthroned forever as a righteous judge.

❖² The Lord rules the world with righteousness and judges the people with equity. God will be a stronghold for the oppressed and a refuge in time of trouble. Our trust is in your name.

● O Lord, you never forsake those who seek you.

❖³ Sing praise to the Lord in Zion; proclaim God's mighty deeds. The Avenger will not forget the cry of the afflicted. Pity me when I suffer and lift me from the gates of death.

● I will sing your praise and rejoice at Zion's salvation.

❖⁴ The ungodly have fallen into their own traps. The wicked and those who forget God will be given over to the grave. Yet the needy will never be forgotten.

● The Lord will never forsake the hope of the poor.

❖ Rise up, O Lord, do not let the ungodly have the upper hand; let them be judged before you.

✪ Put fear upon the ungodly, O Lord; let them know they are only mortal.

✝ I will give thanks to you, O Lord, with my whole heart; I will tell of all your marvelous works.

Psalm 10

This song of thanksgiving by David is an acrostic poem with stanzas beginning with successive letters of the second half of the Hebrew alphabet. This psalm describes the supreme villain.

✝ Why do you stand far off, O LORD, and hide yourself when trouble comes near?

☉ The wicked persecute the poor, boast of their evil desires, and curse the LORD, but they are trapped in their own schemes.

❖¹ The wicked believe there is no god. Their ways are devious, and they scoff at their enemies, but your judgments, LORD, are far above their sight.

● Rise up, O LORD, lift up your hand and forget not the afflicted.

❖² The deceitful lies and arrogance of the wicked fill the air; they lie in wait to ambush and murder the innocent and prey on the helpless.

● Surely, LORD, you behold trouble and take it into your own hand.

❖³ The wicked say, "God hides God's face and will not notice." Why should they say, "You do not care"?

● The helpless commit themselves to you, for you are the defender of orphans.

❖⁴ Break the power of the evildoers; search out their wickedness until none is left.

● The LORD is King forever; the ungodly shall perish from the land.

❖ Give justice to the orphan and the oppressed, O LORD, so that mere mortals may no longer strike terror in the hearts of the innocent.

☉ O LORD, you hear the desires of the humble; strengthen their heart when they cry out to you.

✝ The LORD is King forever. The ungodly will be banished, and the humble will be heard, and justice will reign.

Psalm 11

In this psalm of confidence by David, God is holy and "other." He is set apart from the world; yet he strengthens the faith of his followers even from his holy temple.

✝ I have taken refuge in the LORD, who is the Righteous One.

◑ I have taken refuge in the LORD; so why would you tell me, "Flee like a bird to the mountains"?

❖¹ See how the wicked bend the bow and fit their arrows to the string? They shoot from ambush at the true of heart.

● I take refuge in the LORD, who is the Righteous One.

❖² If the foundations are destroyed, what can the righteous do?

● The LORD is in the holy temple; God's throne is in heaven.

❖³ God's eyes behold the inhabited world; your piercing eye measures our worth.

● The LORD is in the holy temple; our God is the Righteous One.

❖⁴ The LORD tests both the righteous and the wicked, but abhors those who delight in violence.

● I take refuge in the LORD, whose temple is in heaven.

❖ Upon the wicked God shall rain coals of fire and burning sulphur; a scorching wind shall be their lot.

◑ For the LORD is righteous and delights in justice, and faithful followers will see God's face.

✝ I have taken refuge in the LORD, who is the Righteous One.

Psalm 12

In this national lament, David petitions the LORD to rid Israel of the unfaithful leaders. The first word of this psalm, "Yasha," means "save" or "help." It forms the basis of the Hebrew name of Jesus—Yeshua.

✝ Help us, O LORD; watch over us and save us.

☉ Help us, LORD, for the godly are disappearing from among us; the faithful have vanished from the earth.

  ❖¹ Everyone speaks falsely to each other; with a flattering tongue they speak from a double heart.

  ● Watch over us, O LORD, and save us.

  ❖² O LORD, cut off all the flattering tongues, and close the lips that utter proud boasts! Watch over us.

  ● O LORD, save us from this generation,

  ❖³ Those who say, "With our tongue will we prevail; our lips are our own. Who is lord over us?"

  ● Watch over us, O LORD, and save us from this generation forever.

  ❖⁴ "Because the needy are oppressed and the poor cry out in misery, I will rise up," says the LORD,

  ● "I will give them the help they long for."

  ❖ The wicked prowl on every side when vile and worthless acts are highly prized by everyone.

☉ But the words of the LORD are pure words, like silver refined and purified seven times in the fire.

✝ O LORD, watch over us and save us from this generation forever.

Psalm 13

In this individual lament, David dares to plead with God and demand an answer, resulting in an affirmation of David's faith in God.

✝ Give light to my eyes, O LORD, that I might sing your praises.

☉ How long, O LORD? Will you forget me forever?

   ❖¹ How long, O LORD, will you hide your face from me?

   ● Look upon me and answer me, O LORD my God.

   ❖² How long must I bear confusion in my mind and grief in my heart, day after day?

   ● Give light to my eyes, O LORD my God.

   ❖³ How long, O LORD, will my enemy triumph over me?

   ● O LORD, I will put my trust in your mercy.

   ❖⁴ Give light to my eyes, lest I sleep in death, lest my enemy claim they have defeated me and my foes rejoice that I have fallen.

   ● My heart rejoices because you bring me to safety.

   ❖ I have put my trust in your mercy, O LORD, and my heart is joyful because of your saving help.

☉ I will sing to the LORD, for God has dealt with me richly, and God's bounty is even more than I need.

✝ Give light to my eyes, O LORD, that I might praise your holy name.

Psalm 14

This wisdom psalm by David is sometimes known as the Fool's Creed. Here the term "fool" refers to those with moral and spiritual insensitivity—those who neglect to see God in the world around them and follow his laws. The next psalm, Psalm 15, provides the contrast of a faithful believer.

✝ Those who are wise will seek God's presence in all things.

☉ Only the foolish have said in their hearts, "There is no God."

❖¹ The foolish are corrupt and commit abominable acts; not one of them does any good.

● Where are the wise who seek the LORD?

❖² The LORD looks down from heaven to see if there are any who are wise, if there are any who seek after God.

● The LORD in heaven looks down to find those who are wise.

❖³ Everyone has proved faithless. All alike have turned bad; there is no one who does good, no, not even one.

● The wise seek God's presence in all things.

❖⁴ Won't they ever learn, all those evildoers who eat up my people like bread and who never call upon the LORD?

● Israel's salvation will come out of Zion.

❖ See how they tremble with fear, because God is in the company of the righteous.

☉ They mock the plans of the poor and the oppressed, but the LORD is the refuge for the righteous.

✝ The salvation of Israel will come out of Zion! When the LORD restores the fortunes of the faithful, Jacob will rejoice and Israel will be glad.

Psalm 15

Psalm 15 is a song of Zion by David. Picking up on the theme in Psalm 14, David paints a portrait of a faithful believer and attempts to answer the question, "Who can abide in heaven?"

† The righteous shall abide on God's holy hill.

☉ O Lord, who may dwell in your sanctuary? Who can live on your holy hill?

  ❖¹ Whoever leads a blameless life and does what is right, who speaks the truth from his heart.

  ● Those who do what is right will abide on God's holy hill,

  ❖² Those who do not pass on idle gossip or harm their friend, who do not seek to discredit their neighbor.

  ● Those who do no harm will abide on God's holy hill,

  ❖³ Those who reject the wicked, but honor those who seek after the Lord.

  ● Those who honor the faithful will abide on God's holy hill,

  ❖⁴ Those who stand by their oath, no matter the cost, and do not take back their word.

  ● The faithful ones will abide on God's holy hill,

  ❖ Those who do not lend their money in hope of gain, nor take a bribe against the innocent.

☉ Those who live with this understanding will never be overthrown or put to shame.

† These are the righteous who will abide on God's holy hill.

Psalm 16

In this psalm of confidence, David affirms his dependence on God's presence in his life. This psalm is termed a *miktam*. The term is used for several psalms, but its meaning is unknown.

✝ Protect me, O God, for I take refuge in you. I have said to the LORD, "You are my LORD, my good above all other."

✪ All my delight is in the godly who are in the land, in those who are noble among the people.

❖ 1 But those who run after other gods shall have their troubles multiplied. It is you who uphold my lot,

● O LORD, for you are my portion and my cup.

❖ 2 I will not make a blood offering nor take the names of their gods upon my lips. I am content with my heritage.

● My boundaries enclose a pleasant land, indeed.

❖ 3 I will bless the LORD who gives me counsel; my heart teaches me, night after night. I have set the LORD always before me.

● Because God is at my right hand, I shall not fall.

❖ 4 My heart therefore is glad, and my spirit rejoices; my body also shall rest in hope. For you will not abandon me to the grave.

● O LORD, you will not let your holy one see the Pit.

❖ You will show me the path of life; in your presence there is fullness of joy.

✪ In your right hand, LORD, are pleasures forevermore.

✝ Protect me, O God, for I take refuge in you. You are my LORD, my good above all other.

Psalm 17

This individual lament of David is a prayer for deliverance. We can rest in the assurance of God's love for us because we enjoy a unique relationship with God.

✝ Hear my just cause, O LORD, and heed my cry. Listen to my prayer from honest lips.

☉ Declare me innocent, O LORD; let your eyes see what is right.

❖¹ Weigh my heart, summon me by night, melt me down; you will find no impurity in me.

● I have followed your commands and heeded the words of your lips.

❖² My footsteps have stayed on your path; my feet have not stumbled or slipped from following you.

● I call upon you, for you will answer me. O God, listen to my prayer.

❖³ Show me your marvelous grace, O Savior of all who take refuge at your right hand. Save me from my oppressors and keep me as the apple of your eye.

● O LORD, hide me under the shadow of your wings.

❖⁴ Protect me from evil assaults and enemies who surround me. They have hardened hearts and boasting lips. Arise, O LORD, confront them and bring them down.

● With your mighty sword deliver me from the wicked.

❖ They surround me so as to cast me to the ground. Like a lion greedy for its prey, they lurk in ambush. Deliver me, O LORD, from those who look to this world for their reward.

☉ Deliver me from those who appear to have been blessed with rich food and children and wealth enough to leave for their descendants.

✝ But I know, O LORD, that I will see you face-to-face when I awake; I will be satisfied to behold your likeness.

Psalm 18, Part 1 (Verses 1–19)

Psalm 18 is a royal psalm of David, expressing love and thankfulness to the LORD on the day he was delivered from his enemies.

✝ I love you, O LORD of my strength. You are my rock, my fortress, and my deliverer.

✿ My God, you are the rock who keeps me safe, my shield, and my salvation; you are my refuge worthy of praise.

❖¹ The breakers of death rolled over me, bringing fear of oblivion. Cords of hell entangled me; the snare of death was set for me.

● I called to the LORD in my distress; I cried to my God for help.

❖² The earth reeled and the foundations rocked because of God's anger. Smoke rose, and a consuming fire lit burning coals that spewed forth from the ground.

● I will call on the LORD to save me from my enemies.

❖³ God parted the heavens and appeared in a storm cloud. The LORD rode on cherubim and the wings of the wind; dark rain clouds gathered to veil the LORD's approach.

● God heard my voice and listened to my cry of anguish.

❖⁴ From the brightness of God's presence, through a hailstorm, the voice of the LORD Most High thundered from heaven. Arrows of lightning and deep thunder scattered my enemies.

● God reached down from heaven to rescue me out of deep waters.

❖ At your command, the depths of the seas were uncovered and the foundations of the world laid bare, O LORD.

✿ God delivered me from my strong enemies, for they were too mighty for me. They confronted me in the day of my disaster.

✝ The LORD was my support and brought me to an open place. My God delighted to rescue me.

Psalm 18, Part 2 (Verses 20–50)

This is the second half of a royal psalm of David, expressing love and thankfulness to the LORD on the day he was delivered from his enemies.

† The LORD has rewarded my righteousness and clean hands, because I show no offense. I keep your ways, see your judgments, and know your decrees. I have not sinned against you, O God.

☉ You show yourself faithful, upright, and pure, O God, to those who are worthy; but with the crooked you are wily.

❖¹ You save the lowly but humble the haughty. You are a lamp in my darkness. With you I can defeat armies or scale walls.

● God's perfect way shields the faithful with words of truth.

❖² Our LORD is God, a rock who makes me surefooted like a deer and trains me for battle. You give me a victory shield.

● You gird me with strength and make my way secure.

❖³ You lengthen my stride, keep my steps firm, and strengthen me so I may destroy my enemies and put them to flight.

● Your right hand sustains me; your loving care makes me great.

❖⁴ I destroy those who hate me; they cry out, but no help comes. You have delivered me and made me ruler of nations. A foreign people will lose heart and obey me. The LORD lives!

● Blessed is the LORD our rock! Be exalted, O God of my salvation!

❖ You are the God who gave victory and cast down nations beneath me. Therefore I will extol you and sing praises among the people, O LORD.

☉ You rescued me from the fury of my enemies and exalted me above those who rose against me; you saved me from my deadly foe.

† God multiplies the victories of the king and shows loving kindness to David and his descendants forever.

Psalm 19

In this psalm of praise by David, we see God reveal himself through the glory of all his creation.

✝ The heavens declare the glory of God, and the earth itself bears the handiwork of our LORD.

☉ Day after day and night after night, the heavens tell of the wonders of God.

❖¹ They have no words or language, and their voices are unheard; yet their silence fills the earth, and their message resounds.

● Day and night we can see the splendor of God's creation.

❖² God has made a heavenly home for the sun; it comes out like a bridegroom, rejoicing like a champion. It runs from one edge of the heavens to the other, and nothing escapes its heat.

● The law of the LORD is perfect and revives the soul.

❖³ The laws of the LORD are just and clear; they rejoice the heart and give insight to life. The awe and wonder of God's judgments are clean and true, and they will endure forever.

● The testimony of the LORD is sure and gives wisdom to the innocent.

❖⁴ There is great reward in keeping your laws, which enlightened your servant. LORD, you discern unintentional sins; cleanse my hidden faults, for your judgments are sweeter than honey.

● Your laws are more desirable than much fine gold.

❖ Above all, LORD, keep me from deliberate sins; let them not get control over me. Then I will be whole and sound, and innocent of a great offense.

☉ Let the words of my mouth and the meditation of my heart be acceptable in your sight, O LORD, my strength and my redeemer.

✝ The heavens declare the glory of God, and the earth itself bears the handiwork of our LORD.

Psalm 20

David asks for victory in this royal psalm. Psalms 20 and 21 form a pair. Psalm 20 is a prayer asking for victory for the king, and Psalm 21 records God's answer to this prayer.

✝ O Lord, give victory to the king and answer us when we call.

☉ May the Lord answer you in times of distress; may the name of the God of Jacob defend you and keep you from harm.

❖¹ May God send you help and give you strength and support from the holy mountain Zion.

● May God strengthen you and bring success to all your plans.

❖² May the Lord remember with pleasure all the gifts you have given, your sacrifices and your burnt offerings.

● May God remember all your offerings of love and service.

❖³ We will shout for joy at your victory and raise banners to the name of our God; may the Lord grant all your requests.

● May God grant your heart's desire in the day of your victory.

❖⁴ Now I know that the Lord will save the Anointed; God will answer him from highest heaven and give him victory.

● May God's salvation be seen in all your works.

❖ Some put their trust in chariots or horses, some in armies and might, but we will call upon the name of the Lord our God.

☉ They will crumble, fall down, and perish, but we will arise to stand firm and upright.

✝ O Lord, give victory to the king and answer us when we call.

Psalm 21

In this royal psalm, David offers thanksgiving for victory. Psalm 21 records God's answer to the prayer for the king's victory in Psalm 20.

✝ The king finds joy in your strength, O Lord, and greatly rejoices in your victory!

☯ You have given him his heart's desire; you have not denied any request he made.

❖¹ For you met the king with the blessing of prosperity and set a crown of fine gold upon his head. The days of his life stretched on forever.

● The king asked you for life, and you granted his request.

❖² The king is highly honored because of your victory; you have clothed him with splendor and majesty and the joy of your presence.

● For you, O Lord, will give the king eternal blessing.

❖³ Your hand will find all your enemies; your right hand will seize all those who hate you. The king put his trust in the Lord.

● Because of God's faithfulness, the king will not fall.

❖⁴ You will make your enemies like a fiery furnace at the time of your appearing, O Lord. You will swallow them up in your wrath, and fire shall consume them.

● The king finds joy in your strength and rejoices at your victory!

❖ You will destroy the enemy from the land and remove their descendants from the earth, for they intend evil against you and devise wicked schemes.

☯ Yet they shall not prevail, for you will put them to flight when they see your arrows aimed at them.

✝ Be exalted, O Lord, in your strength; we will sing and praise your mighty power.

Psalm 22, Part 1 (Verses 1–15)

This individual lament of David is read every Good Friday as a part of the liturgy in many churches. Much of the passion narrative of Jesus echoes what we read in this psalm.

✝ My God, my God, why have you forsaken me and moved far from my cry of distress?

☉ O my God, I call out both day and night, but you do not answer, and I find no rest. Yet you are the Holy One, enthroned upon the praises of Israel.

❖¹ Our forefathers put their trust in you; they trusted, and you delivered them.

● They cried out to you in trust and were not put to shame.

❖² But as for me, I am a worm and no man, scorned by all and despised by the people. All who see me laugh at me.

● Our forefathers trusted in you and were delivered.

❖³ All who see me mock me; they sneer at me and shake their heads, saying, "He trusted in the LORD; let him rescue him, if he delights in him." Yet you took me out of the womb.

● You kept me safe on my mother's breast.

❖⁴ Be not far from me when trouble is near and there is no one to help, for I have been entrusted to you since birth.

● You were my God when I was still in my mother's womb.

❖ Many young bulls encircle me; strong bulls of Bashan surround me. They open their jaws at me, like a ravenous lion.

☉ I am poured out like water, my bones disjointed, and my heart is like melted wax. My mouth is dry like broken pottery; my tongue sticks to my mouth; and you lay me in the dusty grave.

✝ Be not far away, O LORD. You are my strength; hasten to help me.

Psalm 22, Part 2 (Verses 1, 16–31)

This individual lament of David continues. This section of the psalm is read every Good Friday as a part of the liturgy in many churches. Much of the passion narrative of Jesus echoes what we read in this psalm.

✝ My God, my God, why have you forsaken me and moved far from my cry of distress?

☯ Packs of dogs close me in, and gangs of evildoers circle around me. They pierce my hands and my feet; I can count all my bones.

❖¹ They stare and gloat over me. They divide my garments among them; they cast lots for my clothing. Be not far away.

● O Lord, you are my strength; hasten to help me.

❖² Save me from the sword and the power of the dog. Save me from the lion's mouth and the horns of wild bulls.

● I will praise your name in the midst of the congregation.

❖³ Praise the Lord, all who are faithful. Let the offspring of Israel rejoice; let Jacob's line give glory. The Lord does not despise the poor and downcast. O God, you do not hide your face.

● When we cry out, O Lord, you will hear us.

❖⁴ The oppressed shall eat and be filled, and those who seek the Lord shall shout praise: "May your heart live forever!"

● I will praise you and fulfill my vows before the great assembly.

❖ All the people of earth will remember and turn to the Lord, and all the families will bow down before God. For the Lord is King and rules over all the earth.

☯ The prosperous will eat and worship, and all who are mortal will bow down. My soul will live for God alone, and my descendants will hear the wonders of the Lord.

✝ They will be known as the Lord's own people when they proclaim deliverance to future generations.

Psalm 23

In Psalm 23, David expresses confidence in God's ability and desire to care for us. The shepherd is a common metaphor used for kings of Israel.

✝   The LORD is my shepherd, in whom I place all my trust.

◐   The LORD is my shepherd; I shall never be in want.

❖¹   You make me lie down in green pastures and lead me beside still waters.

●   O LORD, you are my shepherd in whom I place my trust.

❖²   LORD, you revive my soul. You guide me along right pathways for your name's sake.

●   I will dwell in the house of the LORD forever.

❖³   Though I walk through the valley of deep shadows, I will fear no evil.

●   For you are my companion; your rod and staff comfort me.

❖⁴   You spread a table before me in the presence of those who trouble me.

●   You have anointed my head with oil, and my cup is running over.

❖   Surely your goodness and mercy will follow me all the days of my life.

◐   And I will dwell in the house of the LORD forever.

✝   O LORD, you are my shepherd; in you I place all my trust.

Psalm 24

In this song of Zion, David gives the requirements for entrance into the temple, along with our response to all God gives us. "The King of Glory" is the title eventually applied to Jesus for his return.

✝ The earth is the LORD's and all that is in it, the world and all who dwell therein.

✪ For it is God who founded it upon the seas and made it firm upon the rivers of the deep.

❖¹ Who can go up to the mountain of the LORD? And who can stand in God's holy place?

● Those with clean hands and a pure heart may ascend to the LORD.

❖² Those who have clean hands and a pure heart, who have refrained from vain living and have not deceived others with lies.

● They will receive their blessing from the LORD.

❖³ Such is the generation of those who seek the LORD, who seek your face, O God of Jacob.

● They shall receive a just reward from the God of their salvation.

❖⁴ Lift up your heads, O gates; lift them high, O ancient doors, and the King of Glory shall come in.

● Lift up your head and see the King of Glory as he comes in.

❖ Who is this King of Glory? "Yahweh, strong and mighty, Yahweh, mighty in battle."

✪ Lift up your heads, O gates; lift them high, O everlasting doors, and the King of Glory will come in.

✝ Who is this King of Glory? The LORD of hosts is the King of Glory.

Psalm 25

In this individual lament, David expresses total confidence in God. This acrostic psalm seems to be a collection of individual prayers without a unified theme.

✝ To you, O LORD, I lift up my soul; my God, I put my trust in you. Let me not be humiliated, nor let my enemies triumph over me.

✧ Let none who look to you be put to shame; let the treacherous be disappointed in their schemes.

❖¹ Lead me in your truth and teach me, for you are the God of my salvation; in you have I trusted all the day long.

● Show me your ways, O LORD, and teach me your paths.

❖² Remember, O LORD, your compassion and love from ages past. Consider not my youthful sins but remember your love and goodness. Gracious LORD, you teach sinners in your way.

● You guide the humble in doing right; teach your way to the lowly.

❖³ Your paths, O LORD, are love and faithfulness to those who keep your covenant. For your name's sake, O LORD, forgive my sin, for it is great.

● You teach faithful followers in the way they should go.

❖⁴ Those who follow you shall dwell in prosperity, and their offspring will inherit the land, for you are a friend to those who seek your covenant.

● My eyes look to you, LORD, for you will save me from the net.

❖ Turn to me with pity, O LORD, for I am left alone. The miserable sorrows of my heart have increased; save me and forgive my sins.

✧ Look upon the enemies who hate me. Protect my life and deliver me. Let me not be put to shame, for I have trusted in you.

✝ Let integrity and uprightness preserve me, for my hope has been in you. Deliver Israel, O God, out of all their troubles.

Psalm 26

In this individual lament, David pleads for vindication. Vindication can mean judgment, but it can also mean to declare someone righteous or innocent.

✝ My foot stands on level ground; in the full assembly I will bless the LORD.

✪ Vindicate me, O LORD, for I have lived with integrity; I have trusted in the LORD and have not faltered.

❖¹ Test me, O LORD, and try me; examine my heart and my mind. Your love is before my eyes.

● O LORD, I will walk faithfully with you.

❖² I have not sat with the worthless, nor do I consort with the deceitful. I will live with integrity.

● O LORD, redeem me and be gracious to me.

❖³ I have hated the company of evildoers; I will not sit down with the wicked. Your love is before my eyes.

● O LORD, I will walk faithfully with you.

❖⁴ I will wash my hands in innocence, O LORD, that I may go in procession round your altar, singing aloud a song of thanksgiving and recounting your wonderful deeds.

● LORD, I love the house where you dwell and your glory abides.

❖ Do not sweep me away with sinners or the bloodthirsty. Their hands are full of evil plots, and their right hand full of bribes.

✪ As for me, I will live with integrity; redeem me, O LORD, and have pity on me.

✝ My foot stands on level ground; in the full assembly I will bless the LORD.

Psalm 27

In this psalm of individual confidence, David affirms the power of being in a personal relationship with God.

✝ The LORD is my light and my salvation; whom, then, shall I fear? The LORD is my strength; of whom shall I be afraid?

✪ When evildoers come upon me to devour me, when my enemies and foes attack me, they shall stumble and fall.

❖¹ Even though an army should surround me, my heart will not be afraid. Even if I am attacked, I will trust in God.

● Forever, O LORD, let me dwell in your house and see the beauty of your temple.

❖² In the day of trouble, you will keep me safe. You will hide me in your house and set me upon the high rock.

● When you call, O LORD, I will seek your face and sing music to your name.

❖³ You speak to my heart, saying, "Seek my face." Your face will I seek. Do not hide from me or turn me away. Listen to my voice.

● O LORD, when I call, have mercy on me and answer me.

❖⁴ You have been my helper. Cast me not away; do not forsake me, O God of my salvation.

● Even if my father and mother forsake me, I know the LORD will forever sustain me.

❖ Show me your way, LORD, and lead me on your path. Deliver me not into the hand of my enemies, for false witnesses have risen up against me and speak evil of me.

✪ Where would I be if I had not believed the promises of God? I am confident I will see the goodness of the LORD here in the land of the living.

✝ I will await the LORD's pleasure and strength. I will wait patiently for the LORD who will comfort me.

Psalm 28

Psalm 28 is an individual lament attributed to David. Believers can speak boldly with God since they are assured of their place in his kingdom.

✝ The LORD is my strength and my shield; in God will I trust.

☉ O LORD, I call to you; my rock, do not be deaf to my cry. If you do not hear me, I will become like those who go down to the Pit.

❖¹ Do not snatch me away with the wicked or with the evildoers, those who speak peaceably with their neighbors while strife is in their hearts.

● Hear the voice of my prayer when I cry out to you, O LORD.

❖² Repay the evildoers according to their deeds and according to the wickedness of their actions. According to the work of their hands repay them and give them their just deserts.

● Hear my prayer, O LORD, when I lift up my hands in your holy place.

❖³ The wicked have no understanding of the LORD's doings, nor of God's mighty works; therefore God will break them down and not build them up.

● Blessed is the LORD who has heard the voice of my prayer.

❖⁴ The LORD is my strength and my shield; my heart trusts in God, and I have been helped.

● Therefore my heart dances for joy, and I will praise the LORD with song.

❖ The LORD is the strength of all the faithful and a safe refuge for the anointed.

☉ Save your people and bless your inheritance; shepherd them and carry them forever.

✝ O LORD, you are my strength and my shield; in you I will trust always.

Psalm 29

In this psalm of praise, David issues a summons for all created beings of the divine realm to worship God along with the creation we can see.

✝ All creation shouts out the wondrous beauty and glory of the LORD.

❂ Ascribe to the LORD, you heavenly beings, ascribe to the LORD glory and strength.

- ❖ 1 Give to our LORD the glory due his name; worship the LORD in the beauty of holiness.
- ● All creation shouts out the wondrous beauty and glory of God.
- ❖ 2 The voice of the LORD is upon the waters; the God of Glory thunders across mighty waters.
- ● The voice of the LORD is a powerful voice.
- ❖ 3 The voice of the LORD breaks the cedar trees; the LORD breaks the cedars of Lebanon. God makes Lebanon skip like a calf, and Mount Hermon like a young wild ox.
- ● The voice of the LORD is a voice of splendor.
- ❖ 4 The voice of the LORD splits the flames of fire and shakes the wilderness of Kadesh.
- ● In the temple of the LORD all are crying, "Glory!"
- ❖ The voice of the LORD makes the oak trees writhe, makes the deer to give birth, and strips the forests bare.

❂ The LORD sits enthroned above the flood; the LORD sits enthroned as King forevermore.

✝ The LORD will strengthen the people and give them the blessing of peace.

Month Two

· · • • • • • · ·

Psalms 30–55

Psalm 30

This individual song of thanksgiving by David reminds us that, although we may be tried and sometimes disheartened, God will bring us the joy of his presence.

✝ I will exalt you, O Lord, because you have lifted me up and have not let my enemies triumph over me.

◉ O Lord my God, I cried out to you, and you restored me to health.

❖¹ You lifted me up from the dead, O Lord, and gave me another chance at life.

● Sing to the Lord, you faithful ones; give thanks to God's holy name.

❖² For your wrath endures but the twinkling of an eye, O Lord, but your favor lasts for a lifetime.

● Weeping may linger through the night, but joy comes in the morning.

❖³ While I felt secure, I thought nothing could shake me. When you showed me favor, I was as strong as the mountains. But when you hid your face, I was afraid.

● I cried out, O Lord, and pleaded my case before you.

❖⁴ I cried to you, O Lord. I pleaded with the Lord saying, "What profit is there in my blood if I go down to the Pit?

● O Lord, have mercy. Be my helper when I am in need.

❖ If I go down to the Pit, will the dust praise you or declare your faithfulness?"

◉ You have turned my mourning into dancing; you have removed my sackcloth and clothed me with joy.

✝ Therefore my heart sings to you without ceasing. O Lord my God, I will give you thanks forever.

Psalm 31

This individual lament attributed to David is a prayer of confidence in the ultimate goodness of God to answer our call.

✝ In you, O LORD, have I taken refuge; let me never be dishonored. Listen to me and make haste to deliver me in your righteousness.

⊙ Be my solid rock, a castle and stronghold to keep me safe; for the sake of your name, lead me and guide me. I disregard those who cling to false idols, but I put my trust in you, LORD.

❖¹ I rejoice in your mercy. You saw my affliction, my distress, and did not desert me, but set my feet where I can move freely. Into your hands, O LORD, I commend my spirit.

● For you have redeemed me, O LORD, O God of truth.

❖² Have mercy on me, O LORD, for I am in trouble and consumed with sorrow. My life is full of grief, and my strength fails me. My enemies scorn me, and even my friends avoid me.

● Rescue me from the snare, for you are my tower of strength.

❖³ I am forgotten as if dead or a useless broken pot. For I have heard the whispering of the crowd; fear is all around, and they plot against me, to take my life.

● But I have trusted you, O LORD, for you are my God.

❖⁴ My times are in your hands; rescue me from my persecutors. Make your face shine on me, and in your loving kindness save me. LORD, let the wicked be put to shame and silenced forever.

● Even when I couldn't see you, you still heard my voice when I cried out.

❖ Great is your goodness, O LORD, which you have laid up for those who revere you and put their trust in you. Blessed be the LORD, who has shown me the wonders of God's love.

⊙ Love the LORD, all you who worship God. The LORD protects the faithful but repays the proud in full.

✝ Be strong and let your heart take courage, all you who wait for the LORD.

Psalm 32

In this individual song of thanksgiving, David acknowledges God's gracious and merciful response to our confession and repentance.

✝ Blessed are they whose offense is forgiven, and whose sin is put away!

☉ Blessed are they whose record the LORD has wiped clean, and in whose spirit there is no deceit!

❖¹ When I kept silent about my sin, my body wasted away; I groaned all day long. You disciplined me day and night, and I was drained as in the summer heat.

● Then I acknowledged my sin to you.

❖² O LORD, I did not conceal my guilt from you. I confessed my transgressions.

● And you, LORD, graciously forgave my sins.

❖³ All the faithful will pray to you in times of trouble; when floodwaters overflow, they will not reach those who pray. You are my hiding place, and you save me from trouble.

● You are my hiding place; surround me with songs of victory.

❖⁴ The LORD said, "Do not be stubborn like a horse or mule, needing a bridle to obey.

● I will teach you in the way to go and guide your life."

❖ Great are the trials of the wicked; but your mercy embraces those who trust you.

☉ Rejoice in the LORD, you righteous ones, and be glad. Shout for joy, all you who are true of heart.

✝ Happy are the faithful whose transgressions are forgiven, and whose sin is put away!

Psalm 33

This psalm of praise focuses on methods of Jewish worship. A psaltery is an ancient musical instrument—a ten-stringed harp.

✝ Rejoice in the LORD, you righteous; it is good for the just to sing praises.

✿ Praise the LORD on the lyre and the psaltery. Sing for God a new song and sound a fanfare on the trumpet.

  ❖¹ Righteousness and justice belong to the LORD, whose loving kindness fills the whole earth. The LORD spoke the word and the heavens were made and all the heavenly hosts.

  ● The word and works of the LORD are true and trustworthy.

  ❖² God gathers up the ocean as in a waterskin and stores up the sea. Let all the earth fear the LORD and revere God's holy name. For God spoke, and it came to pass.

  ● Our LORD commanded, and it all stood fast.

  ❖³ The LORD foils the will of nations and the plans of people. But God's counsel stands forever, and God's designs fill the earth. Blessed are the nations and the people who worship the LORD!

  ● The LORD looks down from heaven to behold all humankind.

  ❖⁴ From the heavenly throne God gazes on all who dwell on earth. The LORD fashions the hearts of all people and understands all their works.

  ● Our soul waits for the LORD, who is our help and our shield.

  ❖ Neither a strong man nor a mighty army will deliver salvation for the king. Not even a horse can save or ensure escape.

✿ Behold, the eye of the LORD is upon those who revere and await God's love. The LORD will rescue their lives from death and feed them during famine.

✝ Our heart rejoices in you, O LORD, for we trust in your holy name. Let your loving kindness be upon us, as we put our trust in you.

Psalm 34

David is thought to have written this individual song of thanksgiving when he miraculously escaped death at the hands of Abimelech by pretending to be insane.

✝ I will bless the LORD at all times, whose praise will ever be in my mouth. I will glory in the LORD; let the humble hear and rejoice.

☉ Proclaim with me the greatness of the LORD and exalt God's holy name. I sought the LORD who answered me and rescued me from my fears.

❖¹ Without shame, look to the LORD and be radiant. I call in my affliction, and the LORD hears me and saves me from all my troubles.

● The angel of the LORD surrounds and delivers the faithful.

❖² The faithful who revere the LORD will lack nothing. Young lions may suffer hunger, but seekers of the LORD have what they need. Happy are those who trust in God!

● O taste and see the goodness of our God.

❖³ Come, children, listen to me; I will teach you to revere the LORD. Who among you loves life and desires long life and prosperity? The eyes of the LORD are upon the righteous.

● The ears of the LORD will hear the cry of the righteous.

❖⁴ Those desiring long life should refrain from evil and lying words. They should do good; they should seek peace and pursue it.

● When the righteous cry, the LORD hears and delivers them from all their troubles.

❖ The face of the LORD is against those who do evil, to root out the remembrance of them from the earth. The LORD is near to the brokenhearted and will save those whose spirits are crushed.

☉ The LORD will deliver the righteous from all their troubles. God will keep all their bones so that not one is broken.

✝ The wicked fall prey to their evil and will be punished. God redeems the faithful; none who seek refuge will be condemned.

Psalm 35, Part 1 (Verses 1–12, 27–28)

This individual lament by David is an imprecatory prayer for retributive justice. It may sound harsh to our ears, but such harshness is often a first response to deep wounds.

✝ Fight those who fight me, O LORD; attack those who attack me. Take up your shield and armor and rise up to my defense.

✿ Draw your sword and spear to defend me from my pursuers. Let me hear you say, "I am your salvation."

❖¹ Let those who seek after my life be disgraced and those who plot my ruin fall back and be dismayed.

● Fight those who attack me, O LORD; rise up to my defense.

❖² Let them be like chaff swirling in the wind, stirred up by the angel of the LORD to drive them away. Let their way be dark and slippery.

● Let the angel of the LORD pursue my enemies.

❖³ My enemies have secretly set a trap for me; without cause they have dug a pit to take me alive. Foil their plans, O LORD.

● May they be caught in their net and fall into their own pit.

❖⁴ My very bones say, "LORD, who is like you? You deliver the poor from those who overpower them; you save the needy from those who rob them."

● I will rejoice in the LORD and glory in God's victory.

❖ False witnesses have risen up against me and accused me of crimes I know nothing about. They have repaid me with evil in exchange for the good I have done; my soul is full of despair.

✿ Let all who set their face against me be ashamed and disgraced. But let those who support me sing out with joy and be glad as we cry out, "Great is the LORD, who delights in his servant!"

✝ My tongue will tell of your righteousness and sing your praise all the day long.

Psalm 35, Part 2 (Verses 1–2, 13–28)

David continues his imprecatory prayer for retributive justice. Those who have experienced deep wounds may identify with this psalm's bitter words.

✝ Fight those who fight me, O LORD; attack those who attack me. Take up your shield and armor and rise up to help me.

☯ Draw your sword and bar the way against those who pursue me; say to my soul, "I am your salvation."

❖¹ When my enemy was sick, I wore sackcloth and humbled myself with fasting. I mourned and grieved as if for my mother.

● I prayed with my whole heart as one would for a friend or a brother.

❖² But when I stumbled, they rejoiced and gathered against me; strangers tore me to pieces without ceasing. They tested me and mocked me and gnashed their teeth at me.

● O God, how long till you rescue my soul from the young lions?

❖³ Do not let my enemies rejoice over me or smirk at my misfortune, for they do not plan for peace, but plot deceitful schemes against the innocent in the land. I will praise you, LORD.

● I will give thanks in the great congregation before all people.

❖⁴ They shout to accuse me, "Aha! We saw it with our own eyes." You saw it, O LORD; do not be silent. O LORD, be not far from me.

● Awake, arise to my cause, defend me, my God and my LORD!

❖ Give me justice, O LORD my God, in your righteousness; do not let them triumph over me. Do not let them gloat or say, "We have swallowed him up."

☯ Let all who set their face against me be ashamed and disgraced. But let those who support me sing out with joy and be glad as we cry out, "Great is the LORD, who delights in his servant!"

✝ My tongue will tell of your righteousness and sing your praise all the day long.

Psalm 36

In this individual lament attributed to David, "he" refers to "my enemy." As the psalm progresses, we see the enemy spiraling down into oblivion, regardless of the goodness of God.

✝ Your steadfast love, O Lord, reaches to the heavens, and your faithfulness to the clouds.

✪ There is a voice of rebellion deep in the heart of the wicked, where there is no fear of God. The enemy flatters himself in his own eyes that his hateful sin will continue to be undiscovered.

❖¹ His words are wicked and deceitful; he has stopped acting wisely and doing good. He dreams up wickedness while lying in bed.

● But your steadfast love, O Lord, reaches to the heavens.

❖² He is set on a path that is not good; he makes no attempt to reject evil. Your righteousness is like strong mountains, O Lord.

● Your justice is like the great deep; O Lord, you save both human and beast.

❖³ How priceless is your steadfast love, O God! All people feast upon the abundance of your house and drink from the river of your delights.

● All will find shelter under the shadow of your wings.

❖⁴ Continue your loving kindness to those who know you, and your favor to those who are true of heart.

● In you is the fountain of life, and in your light we see light.

❖ Let not the foot of the arrogant tread upon me, nor the hand of the wicked drive me away.

✪ See how they are fallen, those who love to do evil! They are cast down and shall not be able to rise.

✝ Your love, O Lord, reaches to the heavens, and your faithfulness to the clouds.

Psalm 37, Part 1 (Verses 1–18)

Psalm 37 is a wisdom psalm attributed to David. Even in the face of the apparent success of his enemy, David advocates meekness as strength that comes from trusting God.

✝ Be still before the LORD and wait patiently until God comes.

☉ Do not be upset because of evildoers and do not envy those who do wrong, for they will soon wither and fade away like the grass.

❖¹ Trust in the LORD; do good as you dwell in the land and feed on its riches. Delight in God, who will provide your heart's desire.

● Commit your way to the LORD; trust God to act on your behalf.

❖² God will make your innocence radiate like the dawn and your just dealing shine like the noonday sun. Do not worry over those who prosper because of their evil schemes.

● Be still before the LORD and wait patiently for our God.

❖³ Refrain from anger and leave rage alone, for it leads only to evil. For evildoers shall be cut off, but those who wait upon the LORD shall inherit the land.

● The meek shall indeed delight in the abundance of peace.

❖⁴ Soon the wicked will be no more; you shall search out their place, but they will not be there. The wicked plot against the righteous and gnash their teeth at them.

● The LORD laughs at the wicked, knowing that their day will come.

❖ The wicked raise both sword and bow to strike down the poor and needy and those who are upright in their ways. But their sword will pierce their own heart, and their bow will be broken.

☉ The little that the righteous have is better than the wealth of the wicked; for the power of the wicked will be broken, but the LORD will uphold the righteous.

✝ The LORD cares for the lives of the godly, and their inheritance shall last forever.

Psalm 37, Part 2 (Verses 18–40)

In this wisdom psalm, David continues to advocate meekness as strength that comes from trusting God.

✝ The LORD cares for the lives of the godly. We will not be distressed in hard times, and in days of famine we will have enough.

✷ For the enemies of the LORD shall perish, and their glory shall vanish like smoke. The wicked borrow and do not repay, but the righteous are generous in giving.

❖¹ Those who are blessed by God will inherit the land. When we stumble, we will not fall, for the LORD holds us by the hand.

● Our steps are directed by the LORD, who strengthens us.

❖² In all my years, never have the godly been abandoned nor their children left to beg, for they are generous in lending. Turn from evil, do good, and dwell in the land.

● Do not abandon the faithful, O LORD; your justice will keep them safe forever.

❖³ The law of God fills the hearts of the faithful, and they will not stumble. The wicked spy on the righteous and seek occasion to kill them. But the faithful will inherit the land.

● The righteous will speak of wisdom and justice.

❖⁴ Wait upon the LORD, staying on the path. God will raise you up to possess the land. I have seen the wicked in their arrogance, flourishing like a tree in full leaf.

● Do not abandon the faithful, O LORD, or let them be found guilty.

❖ I searched for the wicked, but they could not be found. Mark the honest and see the upright, for there is a future for the peaceable.

❂ All transgressors will be destroyed, and the future of the wicked is cut off. But the deliverance of the righteous comes from the LORD who is their stronghold in times of trouble.

✝ The LORD will help them and rescue them; God will save them from the wicked and deliver them, because they seek refuge in God alone.

Psalm 38

This individual lament of David serves as a reminder that God's discipline is not punitive but is meant to restore relationship.

✝ In you, O Lord, I fix all my hope; you will answer me, O Lord my God.

◉ O Lord, do not rebuke me in your anger; do not punish me in your wrath. For your arrows have already pierced me, and your hand presses hard upon me.

❖¹ My health fails and my body is weak because of my sin and your accusation. For my sins overwhelm me and have become a burden too heavy for me to carry.

● Do not abandon me, O Lord my God; stay close by my side.

❖² My wounds fester because of my foolishness. I mourn all the day long, because my body is wracked by pain and there is no health in it. Do not let my enemies rejoice when my foot slips.

● Do not let my enemies rejoice at my downfall.

❖³ I am utterly numb and crushed. My pounding heart groans and my strength fails. Even the brightness of my eyes has faded.

● O Lord, you know my longing, and you hear my sighing.

❖⁴ Those who know me draw back from my affliction and stand far off. Those who seek to do me harm set traps for me, speak lies, and plot deceptions all day long.

● O Lord, I confess my sin and ask forgiveness for my guilt.

❖ I have become like the deaf who do not hear; like those who are mute, I speak no defense with my mouth. Those who repay my good with their evil oppose me because I pursue good.

◉ Those who hate me without cause are mighty and many in number. I am on the verge of falling, and my pain is always with me.

✝ Come quickly to help me, O Lord of my salvation. In you, O Lord, I fix all my hope; you will answer me, O Lord my God.

Psalm 39

Psalm 39 is an individual lament in which David acknowledges his confession voiced in Psalm 38. He recognizes his guilt, and he accepts his restored relationship with God.

✝ I said, "I will guard my behavior, so that I do not offend with my words.

✪ I will put a muzzle on my mouth when the wicked confront me." So I was silent and said nothing. I refrained from rash words; but my anger grew unbearable.

❖¹ My heart was inflamed, and while I pondered, the fire burst forth, and then I spoke out.

● Lord, remind me that my days are numbered and life here on earth is fleeting.

❖² My years are short, and my entire lifetime is just a moment to you. Each of us is only a breath of your presence.

● Why should I wait for another? For my hope is in you, O Lord.

❖³ We are like shadows, and in vain we pursue our busy lives; we heap up riches and do not know who will benefit.

● Deliver me from all my sins and do not let fools mock me.

❖⁴ I fell silent and did not open my mouth, for surely it was you who acted. Take your affliction from me; I am worn down by the blows of your hand.

● Hear my prayer, O Lord, and listen when I call to you.

❖ With rebukes for sin you punish me, and you consume all that is dear to me; surely our lives are fleeting.

✪ For I am but a sojourner traveling with you; I am only passing through like my ancestors did. Turn your gaze from me, so I can smile again before I go my way and cease to exist.

✝ Hear my prayer, O Lord, and listen to my cry. Do not turn away from my tears but bring me your peace.

Psalm 40

In this individual song of thanksgiving, David acknowledges God's perfect timing when we are willing to wait patiently on God.

✝ I waited patiently for the LORD, who turned to me and heard my cry.

✪ God lifted me out of a mucky pit of despair and set my feet on a rock, showing me a clear path. God gave me a new song of praise to sing, one that would cause many to trust in the LORD.

❖¹ Blessed are those who trust in the LORD and do not turn to false gods. You have done great things, O LORD my God! I would tell of your wondrous works, but they are more than I can count.

● You make awesome plans for us when no one else cares.

❖² In sacrifice and offering you take no pleasure. You have given me ears to hear that you do not want these offerings, so instead I have said, "Behold, I come." My page in the book of life says,

● I love to do your will, O God; your law is planted in my heart.

❖³ I proclaim what is right amid the congregation, and I speak your peace, O LORD. I speak of your deliverance and your faithfulness, not hiding your righteousness. Do not withhold your mercy.

● O LORD, let your grace and truth keep me safe forever.

❖⁴ For many troubles have surrounded me, and my sins have overtaken me. They are more than the hairs on my head, and my courage fails me.

● Please, O LORD, rescue me; my God, make haste to help me.

❖ O LORD, shame those who seek to destroy my life; let those who delight in my misfortune be disgraced and confused, and let those who gloat over me be ashamed.

✿ Let all those who seek you rejoice in your presence and be glad; let those who love your salvation proclaim your greatness. Even though I am poor and afflicted, still the LORD cares for me.

✝ You are my helper and my deliverer; do not delay, O my God.

Psalm 41

David acknowledges in this individual song of thanksgiving that both body and spirit are in need of redeeming grace. This psalm ends with a doxology and concludes the first book of Psalms.

✝ How blessed are those who care for the poor and needy! The LORD will rescue them when trouble comes.

✵ The LORD preserves them and keeps them alive, so that they may be happy in the land; and God will rescue them from their enemies.

❖ ¹ The LORD sustains them on their sickbed and ministers to them in their illness.

● LORD, be merciful and heal me, for I have sinned against you.

❖ ² My enemies are saying wicked things about me, wondering when I will die and my name be forgotten. Even if they come to see me, they speak empty words.

● LORD, in your mercy, preserve me and rescue me.

❖ ³ All my enemies whisper together about me. Their hearts collect false rumors; they go outside and spread them and plot evil against me.

● LORD, hold fast my innocence and set me forever in your presence.

❖ ⁴ "A deadly thing," they say, "has fastened on him; he has taken to his bed and will never get up again."

● O LORD, be merciful and raise me up, and I shall repay them.

❖ Even my best friend, whom I trusted, who broke bread with me, has lifted up his heel and turned against me.

✵ When my enemy does not triumph over me, then I will know that you are pleased with me.

✝ Blessed be the LORD God of Israel, through all eternity. Amen.

Psalm 42

This psalm is identified as a *maskil*, or instructional poem, of the descendants of Korah. It is an individual lament, seeking an intimate relationship with God. This psalm begins the second book of Psalms.

✝ As the deer longs for streams of running water, so my soul longs for you, O God.

✪ My soul is thirsting for the living God; when can I come to behold your face, O LORD?

❖¹ Tears are my food day and night, while my enemies demand, "Where now is your God?" I pour out my soul when I remember these things.

● I joined the crowd and led them to the house of God, singing songs of joy along the way.

❖² With a voice of praise and thanksgiving, we celebrated the great festival. Why then is my soul downcast? What reason do I have to be discouraged?

● I put my trust and praise in God, whose presence is salvation.

❖³ When my soul is heavy within me, then I will remember you from the land of Jordan, and from the heights of Mizar and from Mount Hermon. One deep stream calls to another over the sound of your waterfalls.

● The sounds of your rapids and waves wash over me.

❖⁴ I will say to the God of my strength, "Why have you forgotten me? Why must I mourn while the enemy oppresses me?" Each day, God pours out his unfailing love.

● At night God's song is with me as a prayer to the LORD of life.

❖ My enemies taunt me all day long, and I feel as if my bones are broken. They mock me, saying, "Where now is your God?"

✪ Why are you so full of heaviness, O my soul? And why do you groan within me?

✝ Put your trust in God; I will give thanks to the one who is my Savior and my God.

Psalm 43

This individual lament encourages us to express all our emotions, our thoughts, and even our deepest disappointments to God.

✝ Give judgment for me, O God, and defend my cause against an ungodly people.

✪ Defend my cause, O Lord, and deliver me from the deceitful and the wicked.

❖¹ You are the God of my strength; why have you pushed me aside? And why must I wander around in grief while the enemy oppresses me?

● I put my trust in you, O God of my strength.

❖² Send out your light and your truth, that they may lead me, and bring me to your holy hill and to your dwelling.

● Send out your light, O Lord, to show me your path.

❖³ Then I will go to the altar of the Lord, to the God of my joy and gladness, and I will give you thanks.

● On the harp I will give thanks to you, O Lord, my God.

❖⁴ Why are you so full of heaviness, O my soul? And why are you so disquieted within me?

● Even so I put my trust in you, O God.

❖ O my soul, place your hope in God; for I will sing praise to God once again.

✪ Put your whole trust in the Lord God whose presence brings salvation.

✝ Judge me rightly, O God, and defend my cause. I put my trust in you, my Savior.

Psalm 44, Part 1 (Verses 1–13, 24–26)

This national lament by the descendants of Korah recalls God's saving grace, questions his apparent abandonment, and ends with a plea for deliverance.

✝ Our ancestors have told us, O God, about the deeds you did in their days, in the days of old;

✪ How you drove out the nations and planted our fathers in the land, how you crushed the enemy and made your people flourish.

❖¹ It was not by their sword that they conquered the land; but it was through your right hand and your presence that the land was won, because you favored them.

● O God, you are my King; you command victories for Jacob.

❖² Only through you could we push back our adversaries and trample down our assailants. For I do not rely on my bow, and my sword does not give me victory.

● You, O LORD, give victory over our enemies and shame those who hate us.

❖³ Even though we gloried in you daily, O LORD, you rejected and humbled us, and you no longer go forth with our armies. You made us retreat and allowed our enemies to plunder us.

● Yet, LORD, we will continue to praise your name forever.

❖⁴ You made us like sheep and scattered us among the nations. You sold your people for a trifle and yet made no profit.

● Still, you are the God who commanded victories for Jacob.

❖ You have made us the scorn of our neighbors; we have become a mockery and derision to those around us.

✪ LORD, why do you hide your face and forget our pain and misery? We sink down into the dust, and our body clings to the ground.

✝ Rise up, O LORD, to help us. For the sake of your steadfast love redeem us, O God of our salvation.

Psalm 44, Part 2 (Verses 1–2, 8–9, 14–26)

This national lament by the descendants of Korah continues to recall God's saving grace, questions his apparent abandonment, and ends with a plea for deliverance.

✝ Our ancestors have told us, O God, about the deeds you did in their days, in the days of old;

☉ How you drove out the nations and planted our fathers in the land, how you crushed the enemy and made your people flourish.

❖¹ Even though we gloried in you daily, O LORD, you rejected and humbled us, and you no longer go forth with our armies. You have made us a laughingstock among the nations of the world.

● Yet, LORD, we will continue to praise your name forever.

❖² Daily my disgrace is before me. Shame covers my face because the mockers sling insults, and my enemy is bent on revenge. All this has come upon me.

● Yet we have not forgotten you, nor have we betrayed your covenant.

❖³ Our hearts never turned back, even when you thrust us down into a place of misery and covered us with deep darkness. Our hearts never turned back.

● Our footsteps never strayed from your path, O LORD.

❖⁴ If we have forgotten the name of our God or stretched out our hands to a foreign god, won't you find it out, O God?

● For you, O LORD, know the secrets that reside in each individual heart.

❖ Indeed, because of our faith in you, we are being killed and led to the slaughter like lambs. Awake, O LORD! Why are you sleeping? Arise! Do not reject us forever.

☉ LORD, why do you hide your face and forget our pain and misery? We sink down into the dust, and our bodies cling to the ground.

✝ Rise up, O LORD, help us and redeem us, for the sake of your steadfast love!

Psalm 45

This royal psalm of the descendants of Korah is a love song set to the melody "Lilies." This may refer to David or Solomon as he adorns his bride and prepares for future generations.

✝ My heart is stirring with a noble song; let me recite my verses for the king; my tongue is like the pen of a skilled writer.

☉ You are the handsomest of men, and gracious words flow from your lips because God has blessed you forever. Strap on your sword, O mighty warrior, to appear in your majestic splendor.

❖¹ Your right hand does marvelous things, O mighty warrior; your sharp arrows cause your enemies to lose heart and surrender.

● Ride out to conquer for the sake of truth and justice.

❖² Your throne, O God, endures forever. You rule your kingdom with equity, for you love righteousness and hate iniquity.

● Therefore your God has anointed you with the oil of gladness.

❖³ Your garments are fragrant with spices, and the music from ivory palaces fills the air. Your court includes daughters of kings, and your queen is adorned in gold of Ophir.

● Leave your father, O daughter, for the king desires your beauty.

❖⁴ Bow down to the king who is your master. The people of Tyre, the richest of people, will bring you gifts and seek your favor. All glorious is the princess as she enters.

● The princess wears a gown of golden cloth.

❖ In embroidered apparel she is brought to the king, followed by her bridesmaids. They come with joy and gladness to enter into the palace of the king.

☉ In place of ancestors, O king, you will have sons; you will make them princes over all the earth.

✝ I will make your name known from one generation to another; therefore nations will praise you forever and ever.

Psalm 46

A song of Zion by the descendants of Korah, this psalm was to be played on an *alamot* (a high-pitched instrument). Look for the refrain that appears multiple times: "The LORD of hosts is with us; the God of Jacob is our stronghold."

✝ God is our refuge and strength, a very present help in times of trouble.

☉ Therefore we will not fear, even if the earth gives way and the mountains topple into the depths of the seas.

❖¹ We will not fear, even if the ocean's waters rage and foam, or the mountains tremble at its tumult.

● The LORD of hosts is with us; the God of Jacob is our stronghold.

❖² There is a river flowing joyfully through the city of God, the holy habitation of the Most High.

● God dwells in the city; it will not be overthrown.

❖³ God will help the city at the break of dawn. The nations are in turmoil, and the kingdoms crumble.

● God has spoken, and the earth melted away.

❖⁴ Come now and see the works of the LORD, what awesome things he has done on earth.

● The LORD of hosts is with us; the God of Jacob is our stronghold.

❖ It is God who makes war to cease in all the world, who breaks the bow, shatters the spear, and burns the shields with fire.

☉ "Be still, then, and know that I am God. I will be exalted among the nations; I will be exalted in all the earth."

✝ The LORD of hosts is with us; the God of Jacob is our stronghold.

Psalm 47

Psalm 47 is an enthronement psalm by the descendants of Korah; it is also a messianic psalm that extols God's kingship and hints at a future messiah.

✝   Our God is King of all the earth; sing praises with all your skill.

☉   God has gone up with a shout, the LORD with the sound of the ram's horn.

❖¹   Clap your hands, all you peoples; shout to God with songs of joy. Show reverence to the LORD Most High.

●   The LORD Most High is King over all the earth.

❖²   God subdues the peoples under us and the nations under our feet. The LORD chose a special land as our inheritance.

●   Our inheritance is the pride of Jacob whom God loves.

❖³   God has ascended with a shout of praise, the LORD with the sound of the ram's horn.

●   Sing songs of praise to God; sing praises to our King.

❖⁴   For God is King of all the earth; sing praises with a well-written song.

●   God reigns over the nations, seated on a holy throne.

❖   The nobles of the peoples have gathered together with the people of the God of Abraham.

☉   The rulers of the earth belong to God, who is highly exalted.

✝   God has gone up with a shout, the LORD with the sound of the ram's horn.

Psalm 48

This song of Zion of the descendants of Korah extols Jerusalem as the city of God.

✝ Great is the LORD, and worthy of praise in the city of our God on the holy hill.

✪ It is a beautiful and lofty source of joy for all the earth.
Mount Zion is the very center of the world and the city of the great King.

❖¹ Behold, the kings of the earth assembled and marched forward together. They saw the city and were astounded; they retreated and fled in terror.

● Our LORD has proved to be the city's strong defense.

❖² Trembling seized the enemies with pains like those of a woman in labor; they trembled like ships of the sea when the east wind shatters them.

● Our God is a sure defense for the holy city under siege.

❖³ As we have heard, so have we seen; in the city of the LORD of hosts, our God establishes this city forever.

● Standing in your temple, we meditate on your loving grace, O God.

❖⁴ Your praise, like your name, O God, reaches to the ends of the earth; your right hand is full of justice. Because of your righteous judgements, O LORD,

● Let Mount Zion be glad and the cities of Judah rejoice in you.

❖ Inspect the city of Zion; walk all around her and count the number of her towers.

✪ Consider well her ramparts, examine her strongholds, so that you may tell the generations to come: This is our God.

✝ This God is our God forever. The LORD shall be our guide for all eternity.

Psalm 49

In this wisdom psalm of the descendants of Korah, we are encouraged to view God with the eyes of faith, believing he will ransom our lives.

✝ Hear this, all you peoples; listen, everyone living on earth, you of high and low degree, rich and poor. My mouth shall speak of wisdom, and my heart shall meditate on understanding.

✤ I will incline my ear to the proverb and set forth my riddle upon the harp. Why should I fear troubled days, when enemies surround me?

  ❖ [1] Why should I fear those who trust in their wealth and boast of their riches? We can never ransom ourselves or deliver to God the price of our life.

  ● The price for our ransom is far more than we can pay.

  ❖ [2] For we see that even the wise die leaving their wealth to others. The grave becomes their permanent home for all generations, regardless of their estate.

  ● The price to live forever and never see the grave is too great.

  ❖ [3] Even though honored, they cannot live forever; they, like beasts, will grow old and die. This is the destiny of fools and their followers. My mouth shall speak wisdom.

  ● God will ransom my life and snatch me from death's hold.

  ❖ [4] Like sheep they are destined for death. The godly will subdue them, and their form will melt in the land of the dead.

  ● My heart will meditate on God, who will ransom my soul.

  ❖ Do not be envious if some become rich and their family grows; for they carry nothing away and their fame does not follow them.

✤ Though they thought highly of themselves while they lived and were praised for their success, they shall join their ancestors who will never see the light again.

✝ Those who are honored but have no understanding are like the beasts that perish, but God will ransom my life.

Psalm 50

Asaph speaks in this song of Zion on behalf of God, who is not looking for sacrifices, but desires true worship and thanksgiving.

✝ Our mighty God has spoken and calls to the earth from sunrise to sunset. Out of Zion, in perfect beauty, God reveals majestic glory.

⊙ Our God comes, not in silence, but with a consuming flame and a raging storm. God calls heaven and earth to come judge all people.

❖¹ "Gather before me, faithful ones who have made a covenant and sealed it with sacrifice." The heavens declare the righteousness of God who is judge. God speaks to the faithful:

● "O Israel, I will bear witness against you; for I am your God.

❖² Not because of your sacrifices, for your offerings are always before me. I do not need bulls or goats from your pens; for all beasts of the forest and the cattle on the hill are mine.

● All birds of the air and all creatures of the field belong to me.

❖³ If I were hungry, would I tell you? For the whole world and all therein is mine. Do you think I eat the flesh of bulls or drink the blood of goats?

● Offer a sacrifice of thanksgiving and make good your vows to God."

❖⁴ To the wicked, God says, "Why do you quote my law and covenant, since you ignore my words and discipline? I plead my case before you.

● Call on me in times of trouble so I can deliver you.

❖ Consider well, you who forget God, lest I remove your salvation. You make thieves your friend and cast your lot with adulterers. You have spoken for evil and even slandered your brother.

⊙ When I didn't speak, you believed that I thought like you. Now I rebuke you, but to those who obey my will, I show my salvation.

✝ Any who offer me a sacrifice of thanksgiving show honor, and to those who walk in my way I will show the salvation of God."

Psalm 51

Psalm 51 is an individual lament attributed to David, who repents after Nathan the prophet confronts him following his affair with Bathsheba.

✝ Have mercy on me, O God, according to your loving kindness; in your great compassion blot out my offenses.

☉ Wash me completely from my wickedness and cleanse me from my sin. For I know my transgressions; and my sin is ever before me.

❖¹ Against you only have I sinned and done evil in your sight. So you are justified and blameless in your judgment. Indeed, I was born guilty, a sinner from conception.

● O LORD, you look for truth within me and teach wisdom to my heart.

❖² Purge my sin; wash me, and I will be clean. Let sounds of gladness resound so that my broken body may rejoice. Hide your face from my sins and blot out all my iniquities.

● Create in me a clean heart, O God, and renew a right spirit within me.

❖³ Cast me not away from your presence and do not take your Holy Spirit from me. Sinners will return to you, when I teach your ways to the wicked. Sustain me with your bountiful Spirit.

● Give me the joy of your saving help again.

❖⁴ Deliver me from death, O God, and my tongue shall sing of your righteousness, O God of my salvation.

● Open my lips, O LORD, and my mouth will sing your praise.

❖ If you desired it, I would offer sacrifices, but you take no delight in burnt offerings. My sacrifice to God is a troubled spirit; a broken and contrite heart, O God, you will not despise.

☉ Be favorable to Zion, rebuild Jerusalem's walls. Then you will delight in the appointed sacrifices of young bulls on your altar.

✝ Create in me a clean heart, O God; renew a right spirit within me. Give me the joy of your saving help again.

Psalm 52

Psalm 52 is a wisdom psalm in which David affirms the trustworthiness of God's goodness, even in the face of betrayal. "Tyrant" refers to Doeg, a servant of Saul who plotted against David.

✝ I will give you thanks for your mighty deeds, O LORD, and declare the goodness of your name in the presence of the godly.

✤ You tyrant, why do you boast of wickedness against the godly all day long?

❖¹ O tyrant, you plot ruin; your tongue is like a sharpened razor, O worker of deception.

● As for me, I will trust in God's great mercy all day long.

❖² A tyrant loves evil more than good and lying more than speaking the truth.

● But remembering God's great mercy will sustain me each day.

❖³ O you deceitful tongue, you love to hurl words that hurt and tear down.

● The righteous will trust in God's great mercy.

❖⁴ My God will break you down, topple you, and snatch you from your dwelling to root you out of the land of the living.

● The righteous shall see and fear, and they shall laugh at the tyrant.

❖ The righteous will say, "This is the one who did not take God for a refuge but trusted in great wealth and relied upon wickedness."

✤ But I am like a green olive tree in the house of God; I will trust in the mercy of God forever and ever.

✝ I will give you thanks for what you have done and declare the goodness of your name in the presence of the godly.

Psalm 53

This wisdom psalm of David is almost identical to Psalm 14, with only a slight variation toward the end. The other difference is that Psalm 14 often uses "the LORD" (YHWH) where Psalm 53 uses "God" (Elohim) throughout the psalm.

✝ Oh, if only Israel's salvation would come out of Zion! When God restores the fortunes of the children, Jacob will rejoice and Israel will be glad.

☉ The fool has said in his heart, "There is no God."

❖¹ All are corrupt and commit abominable acts; there is none who does any good.

● God looks down from heaven to see if any are good.

❖² God looks to see if there are any who are wise, if there is anyone who seeks after God.

● God looks down from heaven to see if any are wise.

❖³ Everyone has proved faithless; all alike have turned bad. There is none who does good, no, not one.

● God looks down from heaven to find the faithful.

❖⁴ Have they no knowledge, those evildoers who eat up my people like bread and do not call upon God?

● Where are those who seek and call on God's holy name?

❖ See how greatly they tremble! Such trembling has never been seen before.

☉ For God has scattered the bones of the enemy and put them to shame. God has rejected them.

✝ See Israel's deliverance coming out of Zion! When God restores the fortunes of the children, Jacob will rejoice and Israel will be glad.

Psalm 54

This *maskil* of David was to be sung with stringed instruments. It is an individual lament in which David seeks the LORD, rather than revenge, when he is betrayed.

✝ Behold, God is my helper; it is the LORD who sustains my life.

✪ Save me, O God, by your most holy name; in your might, defend my cause.

❖¹ Hear my prayer, O God, and listen to the words of my mouth.

● Save me, O God, by your almighty name.

❖² For the arrogant rise up against me, and the ruthless seek my life.

● In your might, O God, defend my cause.

❖³ The arrogant who are seeking my life have no respect for God.

● Behold, God alone is my helper; the LORD sustains my life.

❖⁴ May God return the evil on those who lie in ambush; in your faithfulness, O LORD, destroy them.

● You, O LORD, are my helper who sustains my life.

❖ Willingly, O LORD, I make my offering to you and praise your holy name, for it is good.

✪ For you, O LORD, have rescued me from every trouble, and my eyes have seen the triumph over my foes.

✝ Behold, God is my helper; it is the LORD who sustains my life.

Psalm 55, Part 1 (Verses 1–16, 24)

In this individual lament, David is lamenting the pain of betrayal by a close friend. He gives voice to his pain by lifting it to God to receive faith and confidence.

✝ Hear my prayer, O God; do not ignore my plea for mercy. Listen to me and answer me; when I find no peace, I call out to you.

✪ I am shaken by the noise of the enemy and the oppression of the wicked, for they create trouble for me and attack me in fury.

❖¹ My heart trembles within me, and the fear of death has overcome me.

● If only I had wings like a dove! I would fly away to safety.

❖² I would flee to find rest in the wilderness. I would hasten to escape from the wind of the raging tempest.

● Confuse their speech, O Lord, for violence and strife rule the city.

❖³ Day and night, watchmen patrol the city walls, but trouble and mischief remain inside while corruption, oppression, and deceit fill the streets.

● But I will call upon my God, and the Lord will deliver me.

❖⁴ It was not an adversary I could bear who mocked me, nor an enemy I could hide from who taunted me. But it was my friend, a trusted companion. We shared sweet fellowship.

● And we walked with the crowd to the house of God.

❖ Let death destroy them suddenly, and let the grave swallow them alive; for wickedness surrounds their home and their heart.

✪ But I will call upon God, and the Lord will deliver me.

✝ I will cast my burden upon the Lord, and my God will sustain me.

Psalm 55, Part 2 (Verses 1–2, 12–23)

David continues to lament the pain of betrayal by a close friend. He gives voice to his pain by lifting it to God to receive faith and confidence.

✝ Hear my prayer, O God; do not ignore my plea for mercy. Listen to me and answer me; when I find no peace, I call out to you.

✪ It was not an adversary I could bear who mocked me, nor an enemy I could hide from who taunted me. It was my friend, a trusted companion.

❖¹ Let death destroy them suddenly, and let the grave swallow them alive; for wickedness surrounds their home and their heart.

● But I will call upon God, and the LORD will deliver me.

❖² Morning, noon, and night, I cry out in my distress, and the LORD hears my voice.

● God will keep me safe and rescue me from my attackers.

❖³ For there are many who fight me. They never change, and they do not fear God.

● God, enthroned of old, will hear me and bring them down.

❖⁴ My companion betrayed his friends and broke his covenant with them. His soft speech hid animosity in his heart. His smooth words hid his drawn sword.

● But you, O LORD, will rescue me from those who attack me.

❖ For you, O LORD, will cast down the bloodthirsty and deceitful to the pit of destruction.

✪ My enemies will not live out half their days. But I will trust you, O LORD, to save me.

✝ I will cast my burden upon the LORD, and God will sustain me. You will never allow the righteous to stumble.

Month Three

......•..•..•..•..•......

Psalms 56–79

Psalm 56

In this individual lament, David realizes that trusting in God can alleviate fear of the world around us.

✝ Have mercy on me, O God, for my enemies are hounding me; all day long they assault and oppress me.

✤ They hound me all the day long; truly there are many who fight against me, O Most High.

❖¹ In God, whose word I praise, in this God I will trust and not be afraid, for what can mere mortals do to me?

● Whenever I am afraid, I will put my trust in you.

❖² All day long they distort my words; their only thought is to harm me.

● I will trust in the LORD and will not be afraid.

❖³ My enemies band together; they lie in wait to spy on me as they seek an opportunity to kill me. Don't let them escape in their wickedness.

● In your anger, O God, bring them down, for I know you are on my side.

❖⁴ You have listened to my sorrows. Store my tears in your waterskin; are they not recorded in your book?

● Whenever I call upon you, my enemies are put to flight.

❖ In God, my LORD, whose word I praise, in God I trust and will not be afraid, for what can mere mortals do to me?

✤ I will fulfill my vow to you, O God, and present you with thank offerings;

✝ For you have rescued my soul from death and my feet from stumbling; now I will walk in your presence, O God, in your life-giving light.

Psalm 57

This individual lament of David recalls the time when David fled from Saul into the cave.

✝ Have mercy on me, O God, have mercy, for I have taken refuge in you.

☉ I will hide beneath the shadow of your wings until this time of trouble has passed.

❖¹ I will call upon the Most High God, the God who is accomplishing a purpose for me.

● From heaven God will send help and save me from my enemies.

❖² I lie in the midst of lions that devour the people; their teeth are spears and arrows, their tongue a sharp sword. To confound those who trample me,

● God will send forth love and faithfulness.

❖³ They laid a net for my feet, and my soul was bowed low; they dug a pit before me, but they fell into it themselves.

● Be exalted above the heavens, O God; let your splendor fill the whole earth.

❖⁴ Wake up, my spirit, awake; with the lute and harp my song will waken the dawn.

● My heart is firmly fixed on you, O God; I will sing your praises.

❖ I will confess you among the nations, O LORD; I will sing praise to you in all the earth.

☉ For your loving kindness extends beyond the heavens, and your faithfulness reaches to the sky.

✝ Be exalted, O God, above the heavens, and let your glory fill all the earth.

Psalm 58

In this national lament attributed to David, the psalmist protests against the unjust rulers of God's people. When civil authorities do not promote justice, one is obligated to take action.

✝ The faithful all cry out, "Surely, there is a reward for the righteous; surely, there is a God who rules in the earth."

☉ Do you, as rulers, indeed hand out just decisions? Do you judge the people fairly?

❖¹ No, you devise evil in your hearts and spread violence in the land. The wicked go astray from birth, telling their lies.

● O LORD, where are the righteous rulers we long for?

❖² They are as venomous as a serpent; they are like a deaf adder who ignores the voice of the skillful charmer.

● Where is the Almighty God who rules this earth?

❖³ Break the teeth and pull the fangs of these young lions, O LORD. Let them vanish like water that runs off.

● Surely, LORD, there is a reward for the righteous.

❖⁴ Let them wither like trampled grass or the snail that melts away. Let them be like a stillborn child that never sees the sun.

● Surely there is a God who rules on the earth.

❖ Before they bear fruit, let them be cut down like a brier; like thorns and thistles let them be burned away.

☉ The righteous will rejoice when they have been avenged; they will bathe their feet in the blood of the wicked.

✝ Surely there is a reward for the righteous; surely there is a God who rules in the earth.

Psalm 59

In this individual lament, David remembers when Saul sent men to watch David's house to try to kill him.

✝ Rescue me from my enemies, O God; protect me from those who rise up against me.

☉ Rescue me from evildoers and save me from those who thirst for my blood. See how they lie in wait for my life.

❖¹ My enemies gather against me though I have committed no offense. As they prepare for battle, O LORD, come to my aid.

● Awake, O God of Israel, show no mercy to the faithless.

❖² The ungodly come forth at night, snarling like dogs and prowling the city. Hear their boasting words that cut like swords, asking, "Who will hear us?"

● But you, O LORD, laugh at them and scoff at the ungodly.

❖³ My merciful God comes to meet me so I may look in triumph on my enemies. Do not slay them, O God my shield, lest we forget; but send them reeling to their knees. My eyes are fixed on you.

● O God, my strength, in you I take refuge.

❖⁴ For the sinful words, the cursing and lying lips, let them be caught in their pride. Make an end of them in your wrath, O LORD, and they shall be no more.

● Let everyone know that the God of Jacob rules to the ends of the earth.

❖ At evening, the sinful return, snarling like dogs and prowling the city. They forage for food and grumble if they are not filled.

☉ But I will sing of your strength and celebrate your love each morning; for you are my stronghold, my refuge in the day of trouble.

✝ To you, O my strength, I will sing praises; for you are my stronghold, the God who shows me love.

Psalm 60

Psalm 60 is a national lament attributed to David after a defeat in the Valley of Salt. The confused jumble of words demonstrates that believers do not have to pray perfectly for the LORD to comfort them.

✝ With God's help we will fight valiantly, for the LORD will trample our enemies under our feet.

✪ O God, you have rejected us and broken us in your anger; now take us back again and restore us to your favor.

❖¹ You have shaken our land and split it open; repair the cracks in it, for the land trembles.

● You have set up a banner for your faithful as a place of refuge.

❖² You have made your people know hardship; we staggered from the wine you provided. Deliver us, O LORD.

● Save your beloved ones by your mighty power.

❖³ God spoke from the heavenly sanctuary, and I rejoiced in the promise: "I will parcel out Shechem and divide the valley of Succoth. Gilead and Manasseh are mine.

● Ephraim is my helmet, and Judah is my scepter.

❖⁴ Moab is my washbasin, on Edom I wipe my sandaled feet, and over Philistia I will shout in triumph."

● Who will bring me into the fortified city of Edom?

❖ Have you not rejected us, O God? You no longer go out into battle with our armies.

✪ LORD, grant us your help against the enemy, for the help of humans is worthless.

✝ With God we will do valiant deeds, and the LORD shall tread our enemies underfoot.

Psalm 61

In this individual lament, David leads his people to pray that the king may be faithful to God. If the king is faithful, then the nation will be secure.

✝ I will sing the praises of your name forever, O LORD, as I fulfill my vows to you each day.

✿ Hear my cry for help, O God, and listen to my prayer.

❖¹ I will call upon you from the ends of the earth when despair is in my heart.

● Lead me to a high rock of safety, O LORD.

❖² For you have been my refuge, a tower of strength to protect me from my enemy.

● O God, let me dwell in your house forever.

❖³ I will dwell in your house forever and take refuge under the shelter of your wings.

● For you, O God, have heard my vows.

❖⁴ You have granted me the inheritance reserved for those who revere your name.

● I will take refuge in the shadow of your wings.

❖ Prolong the life of the king; may his years extend over many generations.

✿ May he be enthroned in God's presence forever, with love and faithfulness to watch over him.

✝ I will sing the praises of your name, O LORD, as day after day I fulfill my vows to you.

Psalm 62

This psalm is an individual prayer of confidence attributed to David. Here David is convinced that if God is our rock and salvation, then he can be trusted with all aspects of our life.

✝ For God alone my soul waits in silence, and from the LORD comes my salvation.

☉ God alone is my rock and my salvation, my stronghold, so that I will never be greatly shaken.

❖¹ How long will this multitude try to crush me, as if I were a leaning fence or a toppling wall?

● O God, you alone are my rock and my salvation.

❖² They seek only to bring me down from my place of honor; lies are their chief delight. They bless with their lips, but in their hearts they curse.

● For you alone, O LORD, my soul in silence waits.

❖³ My hope lies in God, for he alone is my rock and my salvation, my stronghold, so that I will not be shaken. In God is my safety and my honor.

● God, you are my strong rock, and you alone are my refuge.

❖⁴ Put your trust in the LORD only. Important people are only a fleeting breath; even ordinary people cannot be trusted. On the scales they balance out as lighter than air.

● Therefore, we will pour out our hearts, O LORD, for you are our refuge.

❖ Put no trust in extortion, nor pride in robbery; though wealth may increase, do not set your heart on it.

☉ God has spoken once, I have heard it twice, that power belongs to the LORD.

✝ Steadfast love is yours, O LORD, for you reward everyone according to their deeds.

Psalm 63

Psalm 63 is an individual lament of David when he was in the desert of Judah.

✝ O God, you are my God; eagerly I seek you.

✪ My soul thirsts for you, my flesh longs for you, as in a barren and parched land where no water can be found.

❖¹ I have gazed upon you in your sanctuary and seen your power and your glory.

● Your loving kindness is better than life itself.

❖² Therefore my lips will praise you. My soul is content with the feast you provide, and my mouth will sing your praises.

● I will bless you and lift up my hands in your name forever.

❖³ I will remember you upon my bed and meditate on you in the night watches.

● I will praise your name, O LORD, and sing for joy.

❖⁴ You have been my helper, and under the shadow of your wings I will rejoice.

● My soul clings to you; your right hand holds me fast.

❖ May those who seek my life go down into the depths of the earth. Let them fall to the sword and be utterly defeated.

✪ The king will rejoice in God, and all who swear by him will rejoice when the mouths of liars are silenced.

✝ O God, you are my God; eagerly I seek you, for my soul thirsts for you.

Psalm 64

This psalm attributed to David appears to be an individual lament, but it has elements normally associated with a wisdom psalm since it contrasts the destiny of evildoers with that of the righteous. It is a prayer for protection and God's ultimate victory.

✝ The righteous will rejoice in the LORD; they will take refuge and put their trust in God alone.

✪ Hear my voice, O God, when I complain; preserve my life from fear of my enemies.

❖¹ Hide me from the conspiracy of the wicked, from this mob of evildoers. Their sharp tongues are like swords, and their bitter words are like deadly arrows.

● Hide me, O LORD, from enemies who attack me.

❖² They shoot from ambush without warning and without fear. They hold fast to their evil purpose as they plan how to hide their snares.

● Save me, LORD, from the trap that is set for me.

❖³ They say, "Who will see us? Who will find out our crimes? We have thought out a perfect plot."

● Foil their plans, O LORD, so that I might live.

❖⁴ The human mind and heart are a mystery; but God will loose an arrow at them, and suddenly they will be wounded.

● I place all my trust in you, LORD God.

❖ The LORD will make my enemies trip over their own words, and all who see them will shake their heads.

✪ Everyone will stand in awe and declare your wondrous deeds, O LORD; they will recognize and ponder your mighty works.

✝ The righteous will rejoice in you, O LORD, and put their trust in you alone; and all who are true of heart will praise you.

Psalm 65

This national song of thanksgiving by David acknowledges the gifts of God in creation. Regardless of our sinfulness, God provides abundantly.

✝ You are to be praised, O God, in Zion; all our vows to you shall be fulfilled.

☼ To you who hears our prayer, all flesh will come. Our sins are stronger than we are, but you, O LORD, will forgive them all.

❖¹ Blessed are those you choose and draw in to dwell in your courts! We will be satisfied by the beauty of your house and the holiness of your temple.

● O God of our salvation, you answer our prayers with awesome deeds.

❖² Your awesome deeds of righteousness are the hope of all people on earth. You fashioned the mountains by your power and encircled them with might.

● As you calm the waves of the seas, you also calm the turmoil among your people.

❖³ Therefore those who live in the furthest reaches of the earth will stand in awe at your marvelous signs.

● You make both the dawn and the dusk to sing for joy.

❖⁴ You care for the earth and water it abundantly; you enrich the land with water from the river of God.

● You provide a bountiful harvest of grain for the earth.

❖ Soaking its furrows and settling the soil, you soften it with showers and bless its growth. You crown the year with your bounty.

☼ The fields of the wilderness are rich for grazing, and the hills are clothed with joy. Even hard pathways overflow with plenty.

✝ The meadows are clothed with sheep, and the valleys are carpeted with grain. They all shout together and sing for joy.

Psalm 66

This psalm is a national song of thanksgiving. We are all created in relationship with the world, but Israel, despite not always being faithful, was destined to be a light to the world—a prototype for all nations.

✝ Be joyful in the LORD, all you lands; sing praises and glorify God's name in all the earth.

⊙ Say to God, "How awesome are your deeds! Your enemies cringe before your mighty power. All the earth bows down before you and sings praises to your name."

❖¹ God turned the sea into dry land, so we passed through on foot and rejoiced in the LORD who will rule forever.

● Come and see the awesome works of God among the people.

❖² O LORD, you watch over the nations to guard against rebellion. But you allowed us to be caught in the snare, and you laid heavy burdens on our backs.

● God preserves us in life and will not allow our feet to slip.

❖³ You set masters over our heads; we went through fire and water, but you brought us out into a place of refreshment.

● For you, O God, have tested us and refined us like silver.

❖⁴ I will enter your house with burnt offerings and perform my vows, which I promised when I was in trouble.

● Praise our God and make your voices heard around the world.

❖ I will offer you sacrifices of fat beasts with the smoke of rams and oxen and goats. Come and listen, all you righteous, and I will tell you what God has done for me.

⊙ I cried out to the LORD with praise on my tongue. If I had harbored evil in my heart, the LORD would not have heard me.

✝ But in truth God has heard me and attended to the voice of my prayer. Blessed are you, LORD God, for you have not rejected my prayers nor withheld your precious love.

Psalm 67

In this national song of thanksgiving, the psalmist celebrates the fact that God makes himself known and shines his grace into the world.

✝ May the LORD bless us, and may all the ends of the earth stand in awe of our Almighty God.

☉ May the LORD be merciful to us and bless us; O LORD, shine the light of your countenance upon us.

❖¹ Let your ways be known throughout the earth, so that all people may see your saving grace when you deliver your faithful.

● Merciful God, show us the light of your countenance.

❖² Let all the nations praise you, O God; let all the people praise your holy name.

● May the LORD bless us from the ends of the earth.

❖³ Let the nations be glad and sing for joy, for you govern the nations with true justice.

● Let all the people praise you, LORD, and be glad.

❖⁴ You judge the peoples with equity and reach out to guide all the nations upon earth.

● May our LORD God Almighty bless us from Zion.

❖ Let the peoples praise you, O God; let all the people praise your holy name.

☉ The earth has brought forth her harvest, and God, our own God, has blessed us richly.

✝ O LORD God, give us your blessing, that all the ends of the earth will stand in awe of you alone.

Psalm 68, Part 1 (Verses 1–19)

Psalm 68 is a national song of thanksgiving attributed to David. It recalls and rejoices in the mighty works of God.

✝ Arise, O God, and let your enemies be scattered; let those who hate you flee before you and vanish like smoke when the wind blows.

✪ Let them vanish like wax melting in the fire, and let the wicked perish in your presence, O God, but the righteous will be glad and rejoice.

❖¹ We sing praises to your holy name, O God, and exalt you riding on the clouds. You, O LORD in heaven, are the father of orphans and defender of widows!

● Yahweh is your name; we rejoice before you!

❖² Give the outcast a home and bring prisoners into freedom, O God, but cast the rebellious into the dry desert. When you went out before your people and marched through the wilderness,

● The earth shook and the skies poured down rain in your presence.

❖³ At the presence of the God of Sinai, who is the God of Israel, you sent a gracious rain, O God, upon your inheritance and refreshed the weary land. Your people have found a home.

● In your goodness, O God, you have provided for the poor.

❖⁴ The LORD gave the word, and the great company of women bore the tidings. Kings with their armies are fleeing away, but the women at home are dividing the spoils.

● When the Almighty scattered the kings, snow fell in Zalmon.

❖ O mighty mountain of Bashan! O rugged mountain, you look with envy at the hill that God chose as a resting place. Truly the LORD will dwell there forever.

❂ The chariots of God were twenty thousand when God came in holiness from Sinai. You rose on high, freeing captives and receiving gifts even from enemies who feared your dwelling place.

✝ Blessed are you, O LORD God of our salvation, for you lift us up and bear our burdens day by day.

Psalm 68, Part 2 (Verses 19–35)

David recalls the works of God in this national song of thanksgiving. Bloody passages using exaggerated language for reports of victory have been toned down.

✝ Blessed be the LORD day by day, the God of our salvation, who bears our burdens.

✪ Our God of salvation is the one who delivers us from death. But God will crush the heads of enemies who persist in their rebellion.

❖¹ The LORD said, "I will bring them back from Bashan and from the depths of the sea, so everyone will know that victory belongs to the LORD who has utterly defeated the enemy."

● Everyone sees your procession, O God, as it enters the sanctuary.

❖² The singers go before and musicians follow after in the midst of maidens playing tambourines. Benjamin leads and the princes of Judah follow, along with princes of Zebulun and Naphtali.

● Bless God before all people, the LORD who is the fountain of Israel.

❖³ Rebuke the wild beasts, the calves, and the people who lust after silver. Scatter the ones who delight in war.

● Send forth your strength to save us, O God, as you did in the past.

❖⁴ Nobles from Egypt will bring tribute, and Ethiopia will stretch out her hands. Kingdoms of earth will sing praises to the LORD.

● Kings shall bring gifts to you at your temple in Jerusalem.

❖ God rides in the heavens, the ancient heavens, and sends forth a mighty voice for all to hear.

✪ Ascribe power to God whose majesty is over Israel and whose strength is seen in the skies.

✝ How wonderful is God in that holy place! The God of Israel will give strength and power to the faithful, those who are richly blessed by the LORD!

Psalm 69, Part 1 (Verses 1–17)

In this individual lament, David remembers a time when he was falsely persecuted. A consequence of sin is alienation.

✝ Save me, O God, for the waters have risen to my neck. I am sinking in deep mire, and there is no firm ground for my feet.

✪ I have come into deep water, and the floods engulf me. I grow weary crying out for help; my throat is parched, and my eyes have failed to see my God.

❖¹ Those who hate me without cause outnumber the hairs of my head; they would destroy me with mighty lies. Must I return what I never stole?

● O God, you know my foolishness; my sins are not hidden from you.

❖² Let no one who hopes in you be ashamed because of me, LORD God of hosts. For your sake I will endure insults in silence. I am a stranger even in my own house and among my own family.

● Do not let seekers be disgraced because of me, O God of Israel.

❖³ Zeal for your house consumes me; I endure insults that are aimed at you, LORD. I humbled myself with fasting, but they cast insults. When I put on sackcloth, they laugh at me.

● Do not hide but come quickly to answer, for I am in distress.

❖⁴ The drunkards who sit at the gate murmur against me and make up songs about me. But each day this is my prayer to you:

● In your great mercy, God, answer me with your unfailing help.

❖ Save me from sinking in the muck and mud; rescue me from those who hate me, and draw me out of the deep waters.

✪ Do not let the flood of waters wash over me nor let the deep swallow me up. Save me, LORD, from being devoured by the Pit.

✝ Answer me, O LORD, in your loving kindness, and in your great compassion turn to me.

Psalm 69, Part 2 (Verses 18–36)

David's individual lament continues. Look for the differences between David's very human response to persecution and that of Jesus in the passion narratives.

✝ Draw near and redeem me, O LORD: deliver me from my enemies. You see my disgrace and shame and the insults from my enemies.

✿ Insults have broken my inconsolable heart. I look for sympathy, but find none; for comforters, but no one comes. My enemies gave me gall to eat and vinegar for my drink.

   ❖¹ Let their table set with their sacred feast become a snare for them. Let their darkened eyes not see, and make their bodies tremble.

   ● Pour out your judgment upon them, and overtake them.

   ❖² Let their camp be deserted with no one to dwell in their tents, for they continually persecute the faithful whom you discipline.

   ● Hold them accountable for their sins, without vindication.

   ❖³ Erase their names from the book of life so they are not listed among the faithful. Meanwhile, I am suffering, O God; let your saving power raise me up.

   ● I will sing praises, O God, and proclaim your greatness with thanksgiving.

   ❖⁴ This will please the LORD more than an offering of oxen or bulls. The oppressed will see and be glad. Seek God and rejoice.

   ● For the LORD hears the poor and cares for the captives.

   ❖ Let the heavens and earth praise the LORD, also the seas and all that live in them.

✿ For God will save Zion and rebuild the cities of Judah; the faithful will live there and settle in their own land.

✝ The descendants of the righteous will inherit the land, and those who love God's name will live in safety.

Psalm 70

This is an individual lament of David, not unlike Psalm 40, but with more urgency and intensity.

✝ You are my helper and my deliverer, O Lord; do not delay but come quickly to my rescue.

✪ Please, O God, come quickly to deliver me; O Lord, make haste to help me.

❖ ¹ O Lord, let those who seek my life be ashamed and altogether dismayed.

● My God, make haste to deliver me.

❖ ² Let those who take pleasure in my misfortune turn back in disgrace.

● O Lord, do not tarry when I am in need.

❖ ³ Let those who gloat over me turn back, because they are ashamed.

● Let all who seek you, Lord, rejoice and be glad.

❖ ⁴ Let those who love your salvation praise your name forever.

● The faithful praise your name and sing, "Great is the Lord."

❖ But as for me, I am poor and needy; come speedily to my aid, O my God.

✪ Come quickly, O God, to deliver me. Make haste to help me.

✝ You are my helper and my deliverer; O Lord, do not delay, but come quickly to my aid.

Psalm 71

This individual lament expresses confidence that God's mercy is found in all areas of life.

✝ You, O LORD, are my refuge; let me never be disgraced. In your righteousness you have heard my cry; deliver me and set me free.

✪ Be my strong rock, a castle and stronghold to keep me safe. Deliver me, O God, from the wicked, from the evildoer and oppressor.

❖¹ For you are my hope, O LORD God, my sustainer from birth in whom I trust; my praise is always of you. I am a miracle to many because your strength is my refuge.

● My mouth is full of your glory and praise all the day long.

❖² Do not set me aside in my old age when my strength fails. For my enemies conspire together in secret to take my life. They believe you have forsaken me and will not send help to me.

● Do not stay away, O LORD, but come quickly to help me.

❖³ Let my accusers be put to shame, and let those who seek my life be disgraced. But I shall always wait patiently and praise you continually. All day long I will recount your mighty acts.

● I will tell of your saving deeds; they are more than I can count.

❖⁴ I will tell of the mighty works of the LORD God that I have known since my youth. Every day I recount your righteous deeds. Though I am old and gray, O God, do not forsake me,

● I will make known your mighty strength to all generations.

❖ Who is like you, O God? Your deeds and righteousness reach to the heavens. Though I have seen great troubles, you will restore me and bring me up from the deep places of the earth.

✪ You increase my honor and comfort me. Therefore I will praise your faithfulness, O God of Israel, and sing to you with the harp.

✝ I will shout for joy and sing your praises, for my soul has been redeemed by you. I will proclaim your righteousness all day long, because you have put my enemies to shame.

Psalm 72

This royal psalm by Solomon serves as a reminder that we should pray for all those in authority. This concludes the prayers of David, son of Jesse. It is the final psalm in the second book of Psalms.

✝ Give the king your justice, O God, and your righteousness to his son; that he may rule your people fairly and the poor with mercy.

✿ Let the mountains bring prosperity and the hills be fruitful. He will defend the needy, rescue the poor, and crush the oppressor.

❖¹ He will live as long as the sun and moon endure, from age to age. May the king's rule be like showers that water the earth. During his reign let the godly flourish.

● Let peace abide until the moon no longer shines.

❖² He shall rule from sea to sea, from the river to the ends of the earth. Nomads will bow down, and his enemies will fall to dust.

● All kings shall bow down before him, and their people shall serve him.

❖³ The kings of Tarshish will pay tribute and the kings of Arabia and Seba bring gifts. For he shall deliver the poor who cry out and the oppressed who have no helper.

● He will have pity on the poor and save the lives of the needy.

❖⁴ He will redeem them from oppression and violence, for he values their lives. Long may he live to receive gold from Arabia.

● May the people pray for him and give blessings all day long.

❖ May there be abundance of grain on the earth growing thick on the hilltops; may it flourish like Lebanon, and people blossom like grass upon the earth.

✿ May his name remain forever, as long as the sun endures, so that he may bless all nations and they will call him blessed.

✝ Blessed be the LORD God, the God of Israel, who alone does wondrous deeds! Blessed be your glorious name forever! Let the whole earth be filled with your glory! Amen. Amen.

Psalm 73, Part 1 (Verses 1–15, 28)

This psalm, the first in the third book of Psalms, is a wisdom psalm of Asaph. God makes it safe for us to voice our complaints so we may perceive an accurate perspective of the world.

✝ Truly, God is good to Israel, to those who are pure in heart.

✪ But as for me, my feet had nearly slipped out from under me, because I envied the proud when I saw the prosperity of the wicked.

❖¹ For they suffer no pain; their bodies are healthy and strong. They do not share in the misfortune of others and are not afflicted by human ills.

● Have I kept my own heart clean in vain, O LORD?

❖² They wear their pride like a necklace and wrap violence about them like a cloak. Their confidence comes from their prosperity, and their hearts overflow with wickedness.

● Truly, those who forsake you will perish, O LORD.

❖³ They scoff and speak maliciously; in their arrogance they plan oppression. They speak as if they rule in heaven, and their words lay claim to all the earth.

● O LORD, how can people find no fault in them?

❖⁴ And so the people turn to them and drink in all their words. They say, "How does God know? Does the Most High really know what is happening?"

● I know you, O LORD, your right hand holds me fast.

❖ So then, these are the wicked, enjoying a life of ease as their wealth increases. In vain have I kept my heart clean and washed my hands in innocence.

✪ I have been afflicted all day long and chastened every morning. If I had publicized these thoughts, I would have betrayed this generation of your children.

✝ But your presence, O LORD, is all I need. I have made you my refuge, and I will speak of all your wondrous works at the gates of Zion.

Psalm 73, Part 2 (Verses 1, 16–28)

This wisdom psalm of Asaph continues to show that God's goodness makes it safe for us to voice our complaints to God, by which we may receive an accurate perspective of the world.

✝ Truly, God is good to Israel, to those who are pure in heart.

✪ When I tried to understand why the evil ones prosper, it was too hard for me, until I entered the sanctuary of God and discerned the destiny of the wicked.

❖¹ Surely, you set them on a slippery path; you allow them to fall and be swept away to certain destruction in a terrifying end.

● You are my strength, O Lord, and you will keep me safe.

❖² When you arise, O Lord, you will scoff at the memory of them as a person laughs at dreams in the morning.

● Be my guide and my counsel, O Lord my God.

❖³ When my mind became embittered, I was sorely wounded in my heart. I was foolish and ignorant, and I behaved like a brute beast in your presence.

● Yet I am always with you; you hold me fast by my right hand.

❖⁴ Your wise advice will guide me, and afterward, O Lord, you bring me to a place of honor. Whom do I have in heaven but you, O Lord?

● Having you in my presence, I desire nothing upon earth.

❖ My health may fail, and my heart may grow weak, but you, O Lord, are my strength and my portion forever.

✪ Truly, those who forsake you will perish and you silence all who are unfaithful. But your presence, O Lord, is my delight and salvation.

✝ I have made you my refuge, O Lord, and I will declare all your wondrous works.

Psalm 74

This psalm, a national lament of Asaph, provides an example of trusting God even when your world is falling apart.

✝ O God, why have you cast us off? Why does your anger burn against your sheep? Remember the people you purchased long ago.

✪ Remember the tribe you redeemed to be your inheritance and Mount Zion where you dwell. Walk through the endless ruins and see where the enemy destroyed your sanctuary.

❖¹ With a great shout, your enemies entered the temple and set up their victory banners. They hacked the trellis and your carved works with hatchets and axes, then set fire to your sanctuary.

● How long, O God, will the enemy blaspheme your name?

❖² They defiled and burned down all your sanctuaries. No sign or prophet remains, and we see no end in sight. Why are you still, O God? Unleash your right hand to destroy them.

● Yet God, who is the Ancient One, brings salvation to the earth.

❖³ LORD, you split open the sea and shattered the heads of dragons; you gave Leviathan to the people of the desert for food. You have power to split open springs and dry up ever-flowing rivers.

● Day and night belong to you, LORD, also the moon and the sun.

❖⁴ You set up the boundaries of the earth and created both summer and winter. Remember, O LORD, how the enemy scoffs, how a foolish people despise your name.

● Remember your covenant, O LORD, and the plight of the poor.

❖ Do not hand over the soul of your dove to wild beasts in the hidden places of violence. Do not let the oppressed retreat in disgrace.

⊙ Let the poor and needy praise your name, O God. Arise now and defend your cause when you remember how fools mock you all day long.

✝ Forget not the clamor of your adversaries and their unending tumult. Both day and night belong to you, O God of my salvation.

Psalm 75

This wisdom psalm of Asaph testifies to the trustworthiness of God. It is written in response to the prayer embodied in Psalm 74.

✝ We give you thanks, O God; calling upon your name, we will declare all your wondrous deeds.

✿ "Though the earth may quake and all its inhabitants are fearful," says the Lord, "I will make its pillars secure."

❖¹ God will say to the proud, "Boast no more," and to the wicked, "Do not display your strength."

● "I will appoint a time," says God; "I will judge with equity.

❖² Do not raise your strength against heaven, nor boast with an arrogant voice."

● Remember that judgment comes only from our loving God.

❖³ Judgment comes from neither east nor west, nor does it come from the wilderness or the mountains.

● Only God judges who will rise and who will fall.

❖⁴ For in the Lord's hand there is a cup full of foaming spiced wine. God pours out the wine, and all the wicked of the earth will consume it down to the very dregs.

● But as for me, I will rejoice forever and sing your praises, O God of Jacob.

❖ When the wicked are subdued, I will rejoice in you, O Lord, and sing your praises forever.

✿ God will bring down the power of the wicked, and the strength of the righteous will be victorious.

✝ We give you thanks, O God; calling upon your name, we will declare all your wondrous deeds.

Psalm 76

This song of Zion by Asaph speaks to the defeat of the Assyrians and affirms a God who resides among the faithful.

✝ God is revealed in Judah; the LORD's name is great in Israel.

☉ You established your house in Salem, and your dwelling place is on Mount Zion.

❖¹ There you broke the flaming arrows, the shield, the sword, and all the weapons of war. You are glorious, O LORD!

● You are more majestic than mountains filled with game!

❖² The strong of heart have been plundered and sink into sleep; none of the warriors are able to use their weapons.

● At your rebuke, O God of Jacob, both horse and rider lay stunned.

❖³ You, O LORD, are to be revered! Who can stand in your presence when you are angry? From heaven you pronounced judgment.

● The earth trembled and stood silent before you.

❖⁴ The world stood still when God rose up to establish justice and to save all the oppressed of the earth. A remnant of anger hung over the land.

● Surely your righteous judgment will bring praise, O LORD.

❖ Make your vow to the LORD your God and keep it. Let all people bring gifts to the Most High God, who is worthy to be revered.

☉ Make vows and bring gifts to the God who humbles rulers and inspires reverence in the kings of the earth.

✝ God is revealed in Judah; the LORD's name is great in Israel.

Psalm 77

In this national lament, Asaph pours his heart out to God, expressing first frustrations, then confidence, remembering God's salvation from oppression at the Red Sea.

✝ I will cry aloud to you, O God, and you will hear me. Whenever I was faced with trouble, I sought the LORD. Raising my hand, I prayed throughout the night.

☉ I meditated on you without tiring; my soul longed for you. When I think of you, LORD God, I am restless and my spirit faints.

❖¹ Sleep will not come; I am troubled and have no words to pray. I remember the past and meditate on your spirit, O LORD.

● The music you send comforts my heart as I meditate during the long night.

❖² Will you reject me, O LORD, and withhold your favor forever? Have your steadfast love and your promises come to an end?

● I will meditate on your works and ponder your mighty deeds.

❖³ Has God forgotten to be merciful? In anger, have you withheld compassion? Then I knew my weakness was in thinking that your mighty hand would ever change.

● I will remember your works and the wonders of long ago.

❖⁴ Your way, O LORD, is holy; what god could compare to you? You are the God who works wonders, and you declare your awesome power among the peoples.

● You, O God, have redeemed the children of Jacob and Joseph.

❖ When the waters saw you, O God, they trembled, shaken to the very depths. The clouds rained down water; the skies thundered; your arrows of lightning flashed all around.

☉ The sound of your thunder roared in the whirlwind; your lightning lit up the world, and the earth trembled. Your way was through the sea, through the great waters that hid your footsteps.

✝ You, O LORD, led your people like a flock under the care of your servants, Moses and Aaron.

Psalm 78, Part 1 (Verses 1–18, 22)

This historical psalm of Asaph recounts God's actions in Egypt and coming through the Red Sea.

✝ Hear my teaching, O my people; listen to my words. I will open my mouth in a parable and declare the mysteries of ancient times.

☉ Our ancestors shared the great deeds, and we did not hide them from future generations but told of the power and wonders of the LORD.

❖¹ God gave instructions to Jacob and established a law in Israel that they should teach their children, so generations to come might know and instruct their children yet unborn.

● Always teach the next generation the wonders of our God.

❖² Teach them so they might put their trust in God and not forget the wondrous deeds, but keep God's commandments, and not be like their ancestors who rebelled against the Most High.

● They were a generation whose spirit was not faithful to God.

❖³ The people of Ephraim, armed with the bow, retreated in the day of battle and did not keep God's covenant or law.

● They forgot the miracles God had shown them.

❖⁴ The LORD performed amazing deeds in the sight of their ancestors, in the plain of Zoan in Egypt. God split open the sea and made the waters stand up like walls to let them pass.

● God led them with a cloud by day and a glow of fire by night.

❖ God split the hard rocks in the wilderness and let them drink abundantly from the great deep. Our LORD brought forth streams from the cliffs, and the waters flowed out like rivers.

☉ But they went on sinning, rebelling in the desert against the Most High. They tested God in their hearts and demanded food for their craving.

✝ For they had no faith in God and did not trust in God's mighty saving power. Hear my teaching, O my people, listen to my words.

Psalm 78, Part 2 (Verses 19–39)

Asaph's historical psalm continues to recount when the Israelites rebelled in the desert.

✝ The Israelites had no faith and did not trust God's saving power. They insulted God, saying, "Can God set a table in the wilderness?

❍ True, God struck the rock, the waters gushed forth overflowing; but is God able to provide bread or meat for the people?" When the LORD heard this, God's mighty wrath was kindled.

❖ 1 A fire was kindled against Jacob, and God's anger mounted against Israel. So the LORD opened the doors of heaven and rained down manna, giving them heavenly grain to eat.

● So mortals ate the bread of angels; God provided food enough.

❖ 2 The LORD guided the winds from east and south and rained down meat like dust; birds as plentiful as grains of sand fell in the midst of their camp and around their dwellings.

● So they ate and were filled; God gave them what they craved.

❖ 3 Their craving did not stop, though they had food enough. So God's anger flared, slaying the strongest men and subduing the youth of Israel. Even so they continued to sin.

● They had no faith and did not believe in God's wonders.

❖ 4 So God brought their days to a futile end and their years to dismay. Whenever death came, then they would search for the LORD and remember that God was their rock and their redeemer.

● God was merciful to forgive their sins and not destroy them.

❖ But they deceived God, and their tongues were full of lies. Their hearts were not steadfast, and they were not faithful to God's covenant.

❍ Yet God was merciful, holding back anger time after time and not allowing the LORD's wrath to be roused.

✝ For God remembered that they were but flesh, like a breath of air that goes forth and does not return.

Psalm 78, Part 3 (Verses 40–56)

In this section of his historical psalm, Asaph recounts God's saving grace in Egypt, the desert, and even into the promised land.

✝ The Israelites disobeyed and offended God in the wilderness and the desert! Time and again they tested God, the Holy One of Israel.

☉ They did not remember God's power over the enemy, nor the signs God wrought in Egypt, nor the miracles in the plain of Zoan.

❖[1] The LORD turned Egypt's rivers into blood, so there was no water to drink; then God sent swarms of flies and frogs to wreak havoc.

● The people of God forgot the miracles performed in Egypt.

❖[2] God gave Egypt's crops to the caterpillar and the locust. Their vines were destroyed by hail and their sycamores with frost.

● But the people of God did not remember God's works in Egypt.

❖[3] Hailstones and thunderbolts destroyed all Egypt's livestock. God poured out anger and sent a company of destroying angels.

● The LORD bought God's people freedom from Pharaoh with miracles.

❖[4] God sent a plague and in anger did not spare the Egyptians' souls from death. God struck down all the firstborn of Egypt, in the dwellings of Ham.

● God led the faithful like a flock of sheep into the wilderness.

❖ The LORD led them to safety, and they were not afraid because the sea engulfed their enemies. God brought them to this holy land and the hill country that God had acquired.

☉ God drove out the nations before them and apportioned an inheritance to each tribe; then God allowed the tribes of Israel to settle in the land.

✝ Still the people challenged God, rebelling against the Most High, and they abandoned God's commandments.

Psalm 78, Part 4 (Verses 56–72)

Asaph goes on to recount God's actions when the people continued to rebel even in the promised land.

✝ The Israelites tested the Most High God and did not keep the commandments. They turned away in faithlessness just as their ancestors had. They were as undependable as a warped bow.

☉ They grieved God with their pagan shrines and false idols. When God saw this, in anger Israel was rejected.

❖¹ God abandoned the shrine at Shiloh, the LORD's dwelling among the people. The LORD allowed the ark to be captured; God's glory fell into the adversary's hand.

● In anger God abandoned the precious children to the sword.

❖² The fire consumed their young men, so there were no grooms for the maidens. Their priests fell by the sword, and their widows could not mourn.

● Then our LORD awoke as if from a great sleep.

❖³ The LORD woke like a warrior asleep from wine. God beat back the enemies and put them to eternal shame.

● God chose the beloved tribe of Judah and Mount Zion.

❖⁴ The LORD rejected the tent of Joseph and did not choose the tribe of Ephraim.

● God chose David, a beloved servant of the LORD, and took him away from the sheepfolds.

❖ God built the holy sanctuary as high as heaven and as strong as the earth that he founded forever.

☉ God brought David from tending the ewes to be a shepherd over Jacob, over Israel, his inheritance.

✝ So David shepherded them with a faithful and true heart and guided them with his skillful hands.

Psalm 79

This national lament of Asaph is a prayer for atonement. In desperate times we plead with God to restore relationships, for God is the only one who can bring us hope.

✝ We are your people and the sheep of your pasture; we will give you thanks forever.

☉ O God, heathens have invaded your land, profaned your holy temple, and laid Jerusalem in ruins. They have given the bodies of your servants as food for the birds of the air and the beasts of the earth.

❖¹ They have shed their blood like water throughout Jerusalem, with no one to bury them. We have been mocked by our neighbors.

● Let your compassion be swift to meet us, O Lord.

❖² We are an object of scorn and ridicule to those around us. How long will you be angry, O Lord, and your jealousy blaze like fire?

● Help us, O Lord, for we have been brought very low.

❖³ Pour out your wrath upon the heathens who do not know you and upon the kingdoms that do not call on your name. They have devoured Jacob and destroyed his home.

● Remember not the sins of our forefathers, O Lord, but send us your mercy.

❖⁴ Why should the heathen say, "Where is their God?" Let it be known here and abroad that you avenge the faithful whose blood has been shed. Forgive us our sins for your name's sake.

● Help us, O Lord God; deliver us for the glory of your name.

❖ Listen to the painful cries of the prisoners, O Lord, and by your great might save those who are condemned to die.

☉ Repay our neighbors sevenfold, O Lord, for the insults and scorn they have hurled at you.

✝ We are your people and the sheep of your pasture; we will always give you thanks and praise your name forevermore.

Month Four

• • • • •

Psalms 80–105

Psalm 80

Asaph's national lament is also a testimony. While the past and the future may be clear, present suffering can be perplexing. The vine represents the people of Israel.

✝ Hear, O Shepherd of Israel, you who lead Joseph like a flock; shine forth, for you sit enthroned upon the cherubim.

❂ In the presence of Ephraim, Benjamin, and Manasseh, stir up your strength to save us, O Lord. God of hosts, how long will you be angered despite the prayers of your people?

❖¹ You have given us tears for food and bowls of tears to drink. Our neighbors scorn us, and our enemies mock us.

● O God, let the light of your countenance shine on us.

❖² You have brought a vine out of Egypt; you cast the nations out and planted the vine in their place. You prepared the ground for it; it took root and filled the land.

● Restore us, O God; let your face shine on us and save us.

❖³ The mountains were covered by the vine's shadow and the cedar trees by its boughs. Its branches reached to the sea and its tendrils to the river. Turn now, O God of hosts, look down from heaven.

● Tend this vine, O Lord; preserve what you have planted.

❖⁴ Why have you broken the wall, so that all who pass by pluck off its grapes? The wild boars have ravaged it, and the beasts have grazed upon it. It is burned with fire like rubbish.

● At the threat of your presence, O Lord, our enemies will vanish.

❖ Let your hand be upon the ones you have chosen, the descendants of Adam you have raised up for yourself.

❂ Then we will never turn away from you or abandon you, O Lord; give us life, so that we may call upon your name.

✝ Restore us, O Lord God of hosts; let your countenance shine upon us, and we shall be saved.

Psalm 81

This song of Zion of Asaph gives strong encouragement for the people of God to return to the worship of the LORD.

✝ Sing with joy to God our strength and shout aloud to the God of Jacob. Play a song on the timbrel, the melodious harp, and the lyre.

✪ Blow the ram's horn at new moon, again at full moon, and in the day of our feast. For this is a law in Israel, a rule of the God of Jacob.

❖¹ The LORD laid it as a testimony to Joseph, when he came out of Egypt. I heard the unfamiliar voice saying, "I relieved you of the burden on your shoulder and set your hands free from their load.

● You called upon me in the day of trouble, and I saved you.

❖² I answered you from the secret place of thunder and tested you at the waters of Meribah. Hear my warning, O my people. Let no strange god come among you and do not worship a foreign god.

● O Israel, listen to me, for I am the LORD your God.

❖³ I am the one who brought you out of the land of Egypt and said, 'Open your mouth wide, and I will fill it.' And yet my people did not hear my voice, and Israel would not obey me.

● Oh, if only my people would hear my voice!

❖⁴ So I gave them over to the stubbornness of their hearts, to follow their own desires.

● If only my people Israel would walk in my ways!

❖ I would quickly subdue their enemies and turn my hand against their adversaries.

✪ Then those who hate the LORD would cringe before me, and their punishment would last forever.

✝ But you, my people, I would feed with the finest wheat and satisfy you with honey from the rock."

Psalm 82

This psalm is a national lament of Asaph. It is not clear whether this psalm refers to the gods of other nations, or heavenly beings under God's authority, or to gathered earthly leaders. What is clear is that leaders on earth are responsible for imitating the concerns and judgments of God.

✝ God presides in his own congregation and gives judgment in the midst of the gods:

⊙ "How long will you hand down unjust decisions that show favor to the wicked?

- ❖ 1 Save the weak and the orphan; defend the humble and needy.

- ● Only God is judge in the great congregation.

- ❖ 2 Rescue the weak and the poor, and deliver them from the power of the wicked!"

- ● God's decrees come down from the heavenly council.

- ❖ 3 "You have no knowledge, nor do you understand.

- ● You must save the weak and defend the humble.

- ❖ 4 You walk about as if in darkness, so that the very foundations of the earth are shaken.

- ● Rescue the poor and deliver them from the wicked.

- ❖ Now I say to you, 'You are gods, and all of you are children of the Most High.

⊙ Nevertheless, you will perish like mortals and fall like any prince.'"

✝ Arise, O God, and rule the earth, for you have taken all nations as your own.

Psalm 83

This national lament of Asaph is a prayer that tells God what is happening, reminds God of the salvation he has brought in the past, and appeals to God to transform the offenders.

✝ O God, do not be silent. Do not keep still, withholding your peace, O God. For your enemies are in an uproar, and those who hate you have risen up.

✪ They meet in secret to make shrewd plans against your people and those you protect. They say, "Come, let us wipe them out as a nation so the name of Israel will not be remembered."

❖¹ They have conspired together; they have made an alliance against you: Edom, the Ishmaelites, and the Moabites.

● They have conspired against you, O LORD.

❖² The Hagarenes, Gebal, Ammon, and Amalek; also the Philistines and those from Tyre; the Assyrians also joined to aid the descendants of Lot.

● They have joined together to overcome you, O LORD.

❖³ Do to them as you did to Midian, Sisera, and Jabin at the river of Kishinev, when they were destroyed and left to die at Endor.

● Do again what you did in former times, O LORD.

❖⁴ Make their leaders like Oreb and Zeëb, and all commanders like Zebah and Zalmunna, who plotted to take the fields of God for their own possession.

● Overcome their leaders and drive them out, O LORD.

❖ Like fire that burns down a forest, and like the flame that sets mountains ablaze, drive them out with your tempest and terrify them with your storm;

✪ O my God, make them like whirling dust and like chaff in the wind. Cover their faces with shame, O LORD, so they may turn and seek your name.

✝ Let them be ashamed and dismayed forever, and let their confusion perish. Then they will know your name is Yahweh, and you alone are the Most High over all the earth.

Psalm 84

This song of Zion by the sons of Korah extolls the glory and goodness of God in creation.

✝ O LORD of hosts, blessed are they who put their trust in you.

☉ How lovely is your dwelling place, O LORD of hosts! My soul has a desire and longing for the courts of the LORD; my heart and my flesh rejoice in the living God.

❖¹ The sparrow has found a house and the swallow a nest where she may lay her young near your altar, O LORD of hosts, my King and my God.

● Blessed are they who dwell in your house and sing your praises!

❖² Blessed are they whose strength is in God, whose hearts are set on the pilgrims' way. Those who go through the dry Baca Valley will find it a place of springs.

● For the early rains have covered it with pools of water.

❖³ They will climb the heights and increase in strength until they appear before the LORD God in Zion. LORD God of hosts, hear my prayer.

● Listen to the sound of my voice, O God of Jacob.

❖⁴ Behold our defender, O God, and look upon the face of your Anointed. For one day in your courts is better than a thousand elsewhere.

● It is better to stand in the threshold of God's house than to live with the wicked.

❖ For the LORD God is both sun and shield; God alone is able to bestow grace and glory.

☉ The LORD will not withhold any good thing from those who walk with integrity.

✝ O LORD of hosts, blessed are they who put their trust in you.

Psalm 85

This is a national lament of the sons of Korah. Recalling God's mercies of the past will encourage followers to pray for redemptive salvation.

✝ You have poured out blessings on your land, O Lord. You have restored the good fortune of Jacob.

☉ You have forgiven the iniquity of your people and pardoned all their sins.

❖¹ Lord, you held back your fury and turned away from your fierce wrath.

● Restore us again, O God our Savior; let your anger depart from us.

❖² Will you be displeased with us forever? Will you prolong your anger to all generations?

● Revive us again, O Lord, so your people may rejoice in you.

❖³ I hear the Lord God speaking peace to the faithful people, to those who do not follow a path of foolishness.

● Show us your mercy, O Lord, and grant us your salvation.

❖⁴ Surely salvation is very near to those who fear God, whose glory may dwell in our land. Mercy and truth have met together.

● Righteousness and peace will greet with a kiss.

❖ Faithfulness springs up from the earth, and righteousness shall look down from heaven.

☉ The Lord will indeed grant prosperity, and our land will yield a bountiful harvest.

✝ Righteousness shall go before the Lord as a herald, and peace shall be a pathway for God's feet.

Psalm 86

This individual lament of David is at the same time a song of confidence in the goodness of God.

✝ Bow down your ear, O LORD, and answer me, for I am oppressed and in need.

☉ Keep watch over my life, for I am faithful; save your servant who trusts in you. Be merciful to me, O LORD, for you are my God. I cry out to you all the day long.

❖¹ Bring joy to your servant, O LORD, for to you I lift up my soul. For you, O LORD, are kind and forgiving.

● Great is your love toward all who call upon you.

❖² Listen, O LORD, to my prayer, and hear my voice that calls out for mercy.

● In the time of trouble, I will call upon you, O LORD, for you will answer me.

❖³ There is no other god like you, Adonai, nor any deeds that compare to yours. All the nations you have made will come and bow down, O LORD, and glorify your name.

● You are great and do wondrous deeds; you alone are God.

❖⁴ Teach me your way, O LORD, so I may walk in your truth. Draw me close so I may revere your name. I give thanks, O LORD my God, with all my heart and glorify your name forevermore.

● So great is your love for me that you deliver me from the grave.

❖ The arrogant rise up against me, O God. A band of ruthless men, who have no respect for you, seeks to destroy my life. But you, O LORD, are gracious and full of compassion.

☉ You are a God slow to anger and full of kindness and truth. Turn to me and have mercy upon me; strengthen your servant and save the child of your handmaid.

✝ Show me a sign of your favor, O God, so that those who hate me may see it and be ashamed; because you, O LORD, have been my help and my comfort.

Psalm 87

Written by the sons of Korah, this psalm is a song of Zion, praising the goodness and beauty of the city of God.

✝ On the holy mountain stands the foundation of the city of our God.

☉ The LORD loves the gates of Zion more than all the dwellings in the land of Jacob.

❖¹ I will remember Egypt and Babylon among those who know me.

● Glorious things are spoken of you, O city of our God.

❖² Behold, Philistia, Tyre, and even Ethiopia were all born in Zion.

● All things came out of you, O city of our God.

❖³ Of Zion's residents it shall be said, "Each person was born in her.

● Zion is to be praised as the city of our God.

❖⁴ The Most High God himself established the city and will make it ready."

● Let all things sing your praise, O city of our God.

❖ When the LORD registers the people of the nations, he will say, "These also were born in Zion."

☉ The singers, dancers, and those who play flutes will make music: "All the fountains of life spring up from you."

✝ On the holy mountain stands the foundation of the city of our God.

Psalm 88

This psalm of the sons of Korah is an individual lament. It is said to be a *maskil* of Heiman the Ezrachi. The psalmist utters this cry of despair, trusting in God's presence even when it is not felt.

✝ O LORD, God of my salvation, each day and night I cry to you. Let my prayer enter your presence, and listen to my lamentation.

✪ For my soul is full of troubles that draw me near Sheol. I am viewed as one nearing the grave and beyond help as my strength fades.

❖¹ I am set adrift among the dead, like those lying in the grave, like those you remember no more, who are cut off from your help. Your anger weighs upon me heavily.

● Daily I call out to you for help, O LORD.

❖² You have laid me in the lowest dark depths of the Pit, and all your great waves wash over me. You have made me repulsive to my friends and driven them away; I am trapped with no escape.

● LORD, I stretch out my hands to you for mercy.

❖³ My eyes are blinded by my tears. Do you work wonders for the dead? Will they rise up and give you thanks? Can the darkness speak of your glory?

● But as for me, O LORD, I cry to you for help.

❖⁴ Will your loving kindness be declared in the grave? Or your faithfulness in the place of destruction? Will your righteousness be known in the land where all is forgotten?

● In the morning, O LORD, let my prayer come before you.

❖ So why, O LORD, do you reject me? Why do you hide your face from me? Ever since my youth, I have suffered to the point of death. I feel helpless and desperate.

✪ Your fierce anger has swept over me, and your terrors have alarmed me. They surround me like a flood and enclose me on every side.

✝ My friends and neighbors shun me, and darkness is my only companion. O LORD, God of my salvation, hear me when I cry out to you.

Psalm 89, Part 1 (Verses 1–18)

This *maskil* of Ethan the Ezrachi is a royal psalm. God's promises give rise to prayer.

✝ I will sing of your love forever, O LORD; to all generations I will proclaim your faithfulness. For I am certain that your love is established forever, and your faithfulness endures in the heavens.

✪ You said, "I have made a covenant with my chosen one; here is my oath to David my servant: 'I will establish your line forever and preserve your throne for all generations.'"

❖¹ The heavens bear witness to your wonders, O LORD, and to your faithfulness in the assembly of angels. For who in the skies can be compared to the LORD?

● Who is like the LORD among the gods?

❖² Our God is honored in the council of the angels, great and awesome to all those gathered around. Who is like you, LORD God of hosts?

● O mighty LORD, your faithfulness reaches out all around you.

❖³ You rule the raging sea and still the surging waves. You crush the sea serpent and scatter your enemies with your mighty arm. Both heaven and earth belong to you, O LORD.

● You laid the foundations of the world and all that is in it.

❖⁴ You have made both the north and the south; Tabor and Hermon rejoice at your name. Your mighty arm and strong right hand are exalted.

● Righteousness and justice are the foundations of your throne.

❖ Love and truth accompany your rule. Blessed are those who acclaim you, O LORD, for they walk in the light of your presence.

✪ They rejoice in your name all day and are lifted up by your righteousness. For you, LORD, are the glory of their strength.

✝ And by your favor our might is exalted. Truly, our protection comes from you, O LORD, for you, the Holy One of Israel, are our King.

Psalm 89, Part 2 (Verses 19–36)

This *maskil* of Ethan the Ezrachi is a royal psalm. This section recounts the promises made to David.

✝ You spoke in a vision to your faithful people: "I have raised up a warrior and have exalted one chosen from among the people.

☉ I have found David, my servant, and anointed him with my holy oil. My hand will sustain him, and my arm will make him strong.

❖¹ No enemy shall deceive him, nor any wicked man bring him down. I will crush his enemies and strike down those who turn against him. My faithfulness and love shall be with him.

● David will be lifted high through the power of my name.

❖² I will extend his dominion from the great sea to the river. David will say to me, 'You are my Father.

● You are my God and the rock of my salvation.'

❖³ I will make him my firstborn and the highest of the kings on earth. My loving kindness will be with him forever.

● My covenant will forever remain with David.

❖⁴ I will establish his line forever and his throne as the days of heaven. If his children forsake my law and do not walk according to my judgments,

● I will punish their sins and their disobedience with the lash.

❖ But I will not take my love from him, nor will I be unfaithful to my promise.

☉ I will not violate my covenant, nor change the words I have spoken.

✝ Once for all I have sworn by my holiness, for I will not lie to David. His line will endure forever."

Psalm 89, Part 3 (Verses 35–52)

This is the final section of this *maskil* of Ethan the Ezrachi, a royal psalm. This psalm concludes Book III of the Psalms.

✝ God spoke to the people in a vision, "Once for all I have sworn by my holiness, for I will not lie to David. His line will endure forever.

✤ David's throne will remain like the sun before me. It will endure forever like the moon, that faithful witness in the sky."

  ❖¹ But you have rejected your anointed one and become enraged at him. You have abandoned your covenant with your servant and hurled his crown to the ground.

  ● You have broken through his defenses and left his strongholds in ruins.

  ❖² All who pass by plunder him; he has been scorned by his neighbors. You have exalted the right hand of his foes and made them rejoice at their victory.

  ● You turned back his sword and did not support him in battle.

  ❖³ You have put an end to his splendor and overturned his throne. You have cut short his days and covered him with shame.

  ● How long, O LORD? Will you hide yourself forever?

  ❖⁴ How long will your anger burn like fire, O LORD? Remember how short life is and how frail human flesh is. Can anyone live without seeing death or save themselves from the grave?

  ● Where, O LORD, is the steadfast love you promised of old?

  ❖ Where is the promised faithfulness you swore to David? Consider, O LORD, how your servant is mocked. I carry in my heart the insults of many people.

✤ Your enemies have hurled insults, O LORD, at the feet of your anointed.

✝ Blessed be the LORD forevermore! Amen, I say, Amen.

Psalm 90

Psalm 90 is a prayer of Moses, the man of God. It is also a national lament. Looking at earthly suffering against the backdrop of God's eternal plan of mercy brings hope. Moses finds relief in the eternity of God against the mortality of people. This begins Book IV of the Psalms.

✝ Lord, you have been our refuge from one generation to another.

✪ Before you formed the mountains, before the land and the earth were born, you were God. You have been God for all eternity. You turn us back to the dust, saying, "Return, O children of earth."

❖¹ For a thousand years in your eyes are like the passing day or like a night watch. You sweep us away like a dream, but the morning renews us like the grass.

● The grass flourishes in the morning but fades away each evening.

❖² For we wither at your displeasure and are afraid of your anger. All our days ebb away, and our years die away like a sigh.

● Our sins cannot remain hidden in the light of your presence.

❖³ The span of our life is seventy years, perhaps eighty in strength. Even our best years can be marred by labor and sorrow, but they fly quickly by, and we are soon gone.

● Those who understand the power of your wrath will respect your anger.

❖⁴ Teach us to number our days, O Lord, so that we may grow in wisdom. Return, O Lord, do not delay; be gracious to your servants.

● Satisfy us each morning so we may rejoice in your love all our days.

❖ Give us gladness in proportion to our former misery, good years to replace the sorrowful ones.

✪ Show your works to your servants and your splendor to their children.

✝ Let the graciousness of the Lord our God be upon us. Prosper the work of our hands, O Lord, and make our endeavors successful.

Psalm 91

This psalm is a wisdom psalm. Some consider it to be a messianic psalm because lines from it are used by Satan to tempt Jesus in the wilderness.

✝ You who dwell in the shelter of the Most High, abide in the shadow of the Almighty.

✪ Say to the LORD, "My refuge and my fortress, my God, in whom I trust!" For it is you who delivers me from the snare of the hunter and from the deadly plague.

❖¹ Cover me with your feathers, O LORD, and hide me under your wings; your faithfulness is a shield and bulwark.

● I will not fear the terror of night, nor the arrow that flies by day.

❖² I will not fear the plague that stalks by night, nor the illness that comes at mid-day. Though a thousand or even ten thousand fall at our side, it shall not come near us.

● Surely my eyes will see the judgment of the wicked.

❖³ The Most High LORD will be my refuge and dwelling place. Therefore no evil will befall me and no plague come near me.

● You, LORD, give your angels charge over me.

❖⁴ They guard me in all my ways. They bear me up in their hands, so I do not strike my foot against a stone.

● I will walk among wild beasts and serpents without fear.

❖ You will deliver those who love you and protect those who know your name.

✪ Answer me when I call upon you in the day of trouble, O LORD, and rescue me for your honor.

✝ Give long life to your faithful people; satisfy them and show them your salvation.

Psalm 92

This psalm by an unknown author is an individual song of thanksgiving, a song for the Sabbath extolling the glory of worship.

✝ It is good to give thanks to the LORD and to sing praises to your name, O Most High.

❂ It is good to proclaim your loving kindness early in the morning and your faithfulness at night, to play on the ten-stringed lute, on the lyre, and on the melodious harp.

❖¹ For you have made me glad by your acts, O LORD; and I sing for joy because of the works of your hands.

● Your works are great, O LORD, and your thoughts profound.

❖² The fool does not know or understand that the wicked grow like weeds and the evildoers flourish only to be destroyed in the end.

● But you, O LORD, are to be exalted forevermore.

❖³ Your enemies, O LORD, shall perish, and evildoers will be scattered. But you have exalted my strength like that of a wild bull.

● You have anointed me, O LORD, with luxurious oil.

❖⁴ My eyes have seen the defeat of my enemies, and my ears have heard the cries of the wicked who rose up against me. The righteous shall flourish like a palm tree.

● They will grow and spread out like a cedar in Lebanon.

❖ The righteous who are planted in the house of the LORD will flourish in the courts of our God.

❂ They will continue to bear fruit in old age; they will stay fresh and green,

✝ So they may be a witness to our upright LORD, our rock in whom there is no fault.

Psalm 93

This enthronement psalm of the divine kingdom acknowledges God's reign in heaven and on earth for all eternity.

✝ The LORD our God is King; the Most High stands robed in majesty.

✿ The LORD is robed in majesty and girded round about with strength.

❖¹ Our LORD has made the whole world so sure that it cannot be moved.

● Your throne, O LORD, has existed since the world began.

❖² Your throne was securely established from ancient times. You, LORD, are from everlasting.

● You are our King for all eternity.

❖³ The seas have become a flood, O LORD, and the waters roar like thunder.

● The floodwaters produce powerful waves, O LORD.

❖⁴ Consider the strength of abundant waterfalls and how strong are the breakers of the sea.

● Still, our LORD who dwells on high is greater than these.

❖ Your testimonies, O LORD, and your statutes are reliable and will stand forevermore.

✿ Holiness adorns your house, O LORD, forever and forevermore.

✝ The LORD our God is King; the LORD stands robed in majesty.

Psalm 94

This national lament is a song for Sabbath. When we call on the LORD to right the wrongs we see, then God's vengeance becomes just punishment for sins. When we cry out for justice, our anger is eventually replaced by comfort.

✝ O LORD God the Avenger, reveal your splendor. Rise up,
O Judge of the world; render to the arrogant what they deserve.

☉ How long shall the wicked triumph, O LORD? They bluster
and boast in their insolence. They crush and oppress your
chosen people.

❖¹ They murder the widow, the stranger, and the orphans; they
think that you, the God of Jacob, do not see or care. Consider, O foolish people, when will you understand?

● LORD, you do not abandon your people, nor forsake your
own.

❖² LORD, you created the ear and the eye; do you not hear and
see? You discipline the nations and teach knowledge to all
the world. You know our human thoughts, how fleeting
they are.

● Happy are those you have instructed in your law, O LORD!

❖³ You give them relief in times of trouble, until the wicked are
destroyed. For justice will prevail, and the pure of heart will
be vindicated.

● You rose up, O LORD, to defend me against the evildoers.

❖⁴ If you had not come to my help, O LORD, I would have
retreated into silence. When I thought my foot was slipping,
your unfailing love supported me.

● When doubts or worries fill my mind, your comforting
touch brings joy to my soul.

❖ Can corrupt leaders have any part with you, those who bring
misery by framing evil into law?

✪ They conspire against the righteous and condemn the innocent to death. But you, O LORD, have become my stronghold. You are the rock in whom I trust.

✝ You will turn their wickedness back upon them and destroy the evildoers. You, O LORD God, will silence them forever.

Psalm 95

Psalm 95 is a song of Zion. If you are an Episcopalian and you have spent time reading Morning Prayer, the first seven verses of this psalm, known as the Venite, are very familiar. But you may never have seen verses 8–11, beginning on the final cruciform bead.

✝ Come, let us sing to the LORD; let us shout for joy to the rock of our salvation.

◉ Let us come before God's presence with thanksgiving and raise a loud shout with psalms.

❖¹ For the LORD is a great God, and a great King above all gods.

● In your hands are the caverns of the earth, O LORD,

❖² And the heights of the hills are yours also. The sea is yours, for you made it.

● Your hands have molded the dry land.

❖³ Come, let us bow down and bend the knee, and kneel before the LORD our Maker.

● For you are our God, and we are the people of your pasture.

❖⁴ You are our God, and we are the sheep of your hand.

● Oh, that today we would harken to your voice!

❖ "Harden not your hearts, O people, as your forebears did in the wilderness at Meribah, and on that day at Massah, when they tempted me.

◉ They put me to the test, though they had seen my works. Forty years long I detested that generation and said,

✝ 'This people are wayward in their hearts; they do not know my ways.' So I swore in my wrath, they will not enter into my rest."

Psalm 96

This is an enthronement psalm of the divine kingdom. David may have sung this hymn as he brought back the ark of the covenant to Jerusalem. All enthronement psalms are messianic in nature.

† Sing to the LORD a new song; sing to the LORD, the whole earth.

☉ Sing blessings to the name of the LORD and proclaim the good news of God's salvation each and every day.

❖¹ Declare God's glory and marvelous deeds among the nations and among all peoples. For great is our LORD and greatly to be praised.

● Yahweh is more to be revered than all other gods.

❖² As for all the gods of the nations, they are only idols; but it is our LORD who made the heavens. Oh, the majesty and magnificence of God's presence!

● Oh, the power and the splendor of God's sanctuary!

❖³ Ascribe splendor and strength to the LORD, you families of the peoples. Ascribe honor to the name of the LORD; bring offerings when you come into God's courts. Worship the LORD in the beauty of holiness.

● Let the whole earth tremble before our God.

❖⁴ Tell all the nations that the LORD is King! God made the world so firm that it cannot be moved.

● God alone will judge the people fairly.

❖ Let the heavens rejoice, and let the whole earth be glad. Let the sea and all that is in it resound; let the fields and all they contain celebrate.

☉ Then all the trees of the forest will sing for joy before the LORD, who comes to judge the earth.

† God will judge the world with righteousness and the peoples with truth.

Psalm 97

This enthronement psalm of the divine kingdom exalts the coming messiah as the King reigning on the earth.

✝ The LORD reigns as King. Let the earth rejoice; let the distant shores be glad.

☯ Clouds and darkness are all around him; righteousness and justice are the foundations of God's throne.

❖¹ A fire goes out before you and consumes your enemies on every side. Your flashes of lightning cover the earth.

● The whole world sees your glory and trembles.

❖² The mountains melt like wax at your presence, O LORD, for you are LORD of the whole earth. And all people will see your glory.

● The heavens themselves declare your righteousness, O LORD.

❖³ Let those who worship carved images or delight in false idols be put to shame!

● Let everyone bow down and worship only the LORD.

❖⁴ Zion heard and was glad, and the cities of Judah rejoiced because of your judgment, O LORD. For you are most high over all the earth.

● You, O LORD, are exalted far above all gods.

❖ All you who love the LORD, turn away from evil, for God will protect those who follow faithfully and keep them safe from the power of the wicked.

☯ Light shines on those who live a righteous and godly life, and joy gladdens the souls of those who are pure of heart.

✝ Rejoice in the LORD, all you who are righteous, and praise the holy name of God.

Psalm 98

An enthronement psalm of the divine kingdom, this psalm depicts the messianic kingdom as already being accomplished on earth.

✝ Sing to the LORD a new song, for God has done marvelous things.

⊙ With your right hand and your holy arm, O LORD, you have won for yourself the victory.

❖¹ O LORD, you have made your victory known, and your righteousness is revealed in the sight of all nations.

● You have shown your love and mercy to the family of Israel.

❖² Now all the ends of the earth have seen the victory of our God. Let the whole world make a joyful noise to the LORD.

● Lift up every voice, rejoice, and sing to the LORD.

❖³ Sing praises to the LORD with the harp and a melodious song. Sound the trumpets and the ram's horn.

● Shout with joy before the King who is our LORD.

❖⁴ Let the sea and all that is in it make a loud shout, the land and all creatures who dwell there join the chorus.

● Let the rivers clap their hands to the LORD.

❖ Let the hills ring out with joy before the LORD, who comes to judge the earth.

⊙ In righteousness, God will judge the world and the peoples with equity.

✝ Sing to the LORD a new song, for our God has done marvelous things.

Psalm 99

Psalm 99 is an enthronement psalm of the divine kingdom. The reign of God on earth is established, and we are called to proclaim it abroad.

✝ The LORD reigns as King; let the people tremble with excitement.

☉ The LORD sits enthroned upon the wings of the cherubim; let the whole earth shiver.

❖¹ The LORD is great in Zion and exalted above all people. Let them praise the name of God.

● Great and awesome is our God, who is the Holy One.

❖² Our mighty King, you are a lover of justice, and you have established equity.

● You promote justice and righteousness in all of Israel.

❖³ Proclaim the greatness of the LORD and fall down before God's footstool.

● Great is our LORD God, who is the Holy One.

❖⁴ Moses and Aaron were among the priests and Samuel among those who called upon God's name.

● They called out to the LORD, who answered them.

❖ God spoke to them out of the pillar of cloud; they kept the testimonies and decrees that God gave them.

☉ O LORD our God, you gave them an answer; you were a God who forgave their sins, yet punished their evil deeds.

✝ We will proclaim the greatness of the LORD our God and worship at the holy mountain; for the LORD our God is the Holy One.

Psalm 100 and Psalm 117

No author is identified for either of these psalms. Both are psalms of praise and joy in the LORD, and both are a call to worship. This prayer begins with Psalm 100. As you leave the circle on the repeat of cruciform 1, the last three beads are from Psalm 117.

✝ Be joyful in the LORD, all you lands, and serve the LORD with gladness.

✪ Serve the LORD with gladness and come into God's presence with a song of joy.

❖¹ Know this: Yahweh is the God who made us, and we belong to the LORD.

● We are God's people, the sheep who graze in green pastures.

❖² Enter the gates with thanksgiving; go into God's courts with a song of praise.

● Give thanks to the LORD and call upon God's holy name.

❖³ For the LORD is good. This is our God, whose steadfast love endures forever.

● God's faithfulness continues to every generation.

❖⁴ Make a joyful noise to the LORD, all the earth; worship our God with great gladness.

● Come into God's presence with a song of joy.

❖ Sing praise to the LORD, all the earth; worship our God, all you peoples.

✪ Great is God's steadfast love toward us, for the faithfulness of our LORD endures forever.

✝ Hallelujah! Praise the LORD, all you nations.

Psalm 101

This psalm attributed to David is a royal psalm. Much of this psalm focuses on avoiding people who do not have God's interest at heart and avoiding the things they do.

✝ I will sing praises to you, O LORD, for your great justice and loving kindness.

☉ I will strive to live a blameless life. O LORD, when will you come to my aid?

❖¹ I will walk with integrity of heart even within my own house.

● I will not approve of any wickedness that is set before me.

❖² I hate the evil deeds of faithless people and will have no part in them. I will have nothing to do with perverse people.

● I will avoid every evil or harmful action.

❖³ I will silence all persons who secretly slander their neighbors.

● I will not tolerate an arrogant attitude or haughty heart.

❖⁴ I will look with favor upon faithful people in the land to be my companions and to dwell with me.

● Only those who lead a blameless life will serve with me.

❖ Deceitful people will not be invited to serve in my house, and those who tell lies are not welcome in my presence.

☉ Each day I will silence all the wicked in the land and root out all evildoers from the city of the LORD.

✝ My eyes are upon the faithful in the land, that they may dwell with me and be my servants.

Psalm 102, Part 1 (Verses 1–14)

This psalm is an individual lament. It is the prayer of one who suffers and who in weakness pours out his complaint before God.

✝ Lord, hear my prayer, and let my cry come before you; do not turn away from me in my time of trouble.

✵ Listen to me when I call out to you; hear me and answer my cry quickly.

❖¹ For my days seem to drift away like smoke, and my bones feel scorched. My heart is parched and withered to the point that I have lost all appetite.

● Listen to my cry that comes before you, O Lord.

❖² My body is reduced to skin and bones, and my groaning can be heard by all. I have become like a vulture in the wilderness or an owl among the ruins.

● Do not turn away from me in my time of trouble, O Lord.

❖³ I lie awake and moan like a lonely sparrow on the housetop. My enemies taunt me, and those who scoff at me use my name as an oath.

● Listen, O Lord, when I call out to you in distress.

❖⁴ For the bread I eat tastes like dust, and tears run down my face to mingle with my drink because your anger has cast me aside.

● But even so, O God, you will reign forever as Lord of all.

❖ My days are coming to an end, O God, and I am dried up like the grass. But you, O Lord, endure forever, and your name passes down to all generations.

✵ You will rise up and have compassion on Jerusalem, for the appointed time to show mercy has arrived.

✝ For your servants love the stones of its broken walls and cherish the dusty rubble that remains.

Psalm 102, Part 2 (Verses 15–28)

The psalmist's lament continues. The petitioner finds strength in the promises of God.

✝ The nations will revere your name, O Lord, and all the kings of the earth will respect your glory.

✪ For you, Lord, will reveal your splendor when you rebuild Zion. You respond with favor to the prayers of the homeless and will not reject their plea.

❖¹ Let this be written for a future generation, so that people yet unborn may praise the Lord. For the Lord looked down from the heights.

● From the heavens our God beheld the whole earth.

❖² Our God will hear the groan of the captives and set free those condemned to die, so they may declare in Zion the name of the Lord.

● Let them praise the Lord in the midst of Jerusalem.

❖³ The people gather together, and the nations also, to worship the Lord. God has weakened my strength before my time, and shortened the number of my days.

● I said, "O Lord, do not cut my life short by taking me away now."

❖⁴ O my God, who lives forever, do not take me away in the middle of my youth. In the beginning, O Lord, you laid the foundations of the earth.

● Even the heavens were formed by your hands.

❖ One day they will all perish, but you will endure. They will wear out like a garment; like clothing you will change them, and they will be made new.

✪ But you, O Lord, are always the same, and your years will never come to an end.

✝ The children of your servants will dwell secure, and their offspring will thrive in your presence.

Psalm 103

In this psalm of praise, David reflects on the goodness and faithfulness of God throughout history and into the future.

✝ Bless the LORD, O my soul; let all that is within me bless God's holy name. Praise the LORD, and forget not all God's benefits.

✪ You, LORD, forgive all our sins and heal all our diseases; you redeem our life from the grave and crown us with love and compassion.

❖¹ You satisfy us with good things and renew our youth like an eagle's. You vindicate the oppressed with just decrees. You revealed yourself to Moses and your works to the children of Israel.

● You are gracious and merciful, slow to anger and abounding in love.

❖² You will not always accuse us, nor reward us according to our sins. As the heavens are higher than the earth, so is your mercy great upon your servants. As far as east is from west,

● That far, O LORD, you have removed our sins from us.

❖³ You remember that we are made of mere dust, and our life is like the grass. We flourish like a flower in the field; but when the wind blows, it is gone, as if it had never existed.

● As a father cares for his children, O LORD, so you care for us.

❖⁴ Your steadfast love, O LORD, endures forever to those who revere your name. Your righteousness extends in all generations to those who follow your commandments. You have set your throne in heaven.

● O LORD, your kingship has dominion over everything.

❖ Bless the LORD, all you angels, you mighty ones who do God's bidding and hearken to the LORD's voice.

✪ Praise the LORD, all you hosts of the Most High, all you ministers who carry out God's will.

✝ Bless the LORD, all created things of God's dominion; bless the LORD, O my soul.

Psalm 104, Part 1 (Verses 1–19)

This psalm of praise acknowledges the wondrous majesty of God's created world.

✝ Bless the LORD, O my soul; O LORD my God, how excellent is your greatness! You are clothed in majesty and splendor.

☉ You wrap yourself in light as with a cloak and spread out the heavens like a curtain. You lay the beams of your upper chambers in the waters above.

❖¹ You ride on the wings of the wind atop clouds like a chariot. You send forth the winds as your messengers and flames of fire to serve your purposes.

● You set the earth securely upon its foundations for all time.

❖² You covered the earth with floodwaters, even as high as the mountains. But at your rebuke, at the sound of your thunder, the waters quickly receded.

● They ran down the hills and through the valleys to the places you appointed.

❖³ You set a firm boundary for the seas, so that the waters would not cover the earth again. You caused springs to gush forth in the valleys to become streams that flow between the hills.

● All beasts and wild animals drink their fill to quench their thirst.

❖⁴ Birds make their nests by the streams and sing among the tree branches. You water the mountains from your heavenly home, bringing forth fruit to fill the whole earth.

● You give grass for the flocks and crops to feed humankind.

❖ You bring forth food from the earth, wine to gladden our hearts, oil to soothe our skin, and bread to strengthen our bodies.

☉ The cedars of Lebanon, which the LORD planted, are full of sap. In them birds build their nests, and the stork makes his dwelling.

✝ The high mountains and stony cliffs provide refuge for mountain goats and rock badgers. The moon marks the seasons, and the sun knows where to set.

Psalm 104, Part 2 (Verses 19–35)

The psalmist continues to acknowledge the wondrous majesty of God's created world in this psalm of praise.

✝ The moon marks the passing of seasons, and the sun knows its time and place to set.

✪ You make darkness to be the night when all the beasts of the forest prowl. Young lions roar and seek the food provided by God.

❖¹ When the sun rises, they slip away to lie down in their dens. Then the people go out to labor at their work until the evening comes.

● O LORD, how varied and wondrous are your creations!

❖² In wisdom you have made them all; the earth is full of your creatures. Your great sea is teeming with living creatures too many to number.

● You, O LORD, have made creatures both large and small.

❖³ There are sailors in ships to travel the seas, and the Leviathan you made for the sport of it. All of them rely on you, LORD, to provide food in due season. They gather what you provide.

● They are filled with good things that come from your hand.

❖⁴ If you hide your face, they are terrified; when you take away their breath, they die and return to dust. But you, O LORD, send forth your spirit and they are created.

● In this way, O LORD, you renew the face of the earth.

❖ May your glory, O LORD, endure forever; may you rejoice in all your works. You look at the earth and it trembles; you touch the mountains and they smoke.

✪ I will sing to you, O LORD, as long as I live; I will praise my God while I have my being. Let sinners vanish from the earth, and the wicked be no more.

✝ May my meditations please my God, for I will rejoice in the LORD. Bless the LORD, O my soul. Hallelujah!

Psalm 105, Part 1 (Verses 1–22)

This historical psalm is a reminder of God's work on behalf of the people throughout history.

✝ Give thanks to the LORD; sing praises to God's holy name and make all God's marvelous works known throughout the whole earth.

☯ Glorify God's holy name; let the hearts of those who seek the LORD rejoice. Always seek the LORD and the strength of God's presence.

❖¹ Remember the marvelous wonders that the LORD has done and the judgments of God's mouth, O offspring of Abraham, O children of Jacob, for you are God's chosen ones.

● This is the LORD our God, whose judgments cover the world.

❖² O LORD, you remember your covenant forever, the promise you made to a thousand generations. This is the covenant you made with Abraham and the oath you swore to Isaac.

● God established it as a covenant for Jacob; God made this promise to Israel.

❖³ God gave the land of Canaan as an inheritance to the faithful when they were few in number. When they wandered as sojourners from nation to nation, and from one kingdom to another,

● God allowed no one who came near to oppress them.

❖⁴ God rebuked kings for their sake, saying, "Do not touch my anointed and do not harm my prophets." Then the LORD called for a famine and destroyed the grain for bread.

● God sent a man before them, who was named Joseph.

❖ The LORD sent Joseph, and he was sold as a slave. They restrained his feet in shackles and placed his neck in an iron collar.

✿ Then his prediction came true; the word of the LORD was proved right. The king released him; the ruler of the Egyptians set him free.

✝ Pharaoh set Joseph as master over his house and ruler over his possessions, to instruct his officers according to his will and to teach his advisors wisdom.

Psalm 105, Part 2 (Verses 23–45)

This historical psalm continues to recount God's work on behalf of the people throughout history, here relating the events of the exodus.

† Israel came into Egypt and lived in the land of Ham. God's people were very fruitful, and they grew stronger than their enemies.

☉ The Egyptians' hearts were turned, so they hated God's people and dealt unjustly with them. God sent Moses and Aaron as chosen servants.

   ❖¹ They gave signs and worked miracles in the land of Ham. God sent deep darkness and turned Egypt's waters into blood, causing the fish to die.

   ● But the Egyptians continued to rebel against God's words.

   ❖² Their lands, even the chambers of their kings, were overrun by frogs. Then came swarms of insects and gnats within all their borders. Next there came hailstones and lightning in the land.

   ● Pharaoh rebelled against the LORD God of Israel.

   ❖³ God blasted their vines and shattered every tree in their country. At the sound of God's voice, hordes of locusts came and ate up the vegetation and devoured the fruit of the soil.

   ● Still the Egyptians did not believe or change their minds.

   ❖⁴ God struck down the firstborn of all the people and beasts in their land. God led out the Israelites loaded with silver and gold, and not even one stumbled along the way.

   ● Egypt was glad when they left, because they feared Israel.

   ❖ God spread out a cloud for a covering and a fire to give light at night. They asked, and quails appeared, and God satisfied them with bread from heaven. God opened the rock, and water flowed.

✿ A river flowed into the desert, for God remembered the promise made to Abraham, the servant of God. So the LORD led forth the people with great gladness, and the chosen ones with a joyful song.

✝ God gave the Israelites the land of the gentiles, and they harvested the crops that others had planted, so that they would remember to follow the decrees of the LORD and obey God's instructions. Hallelujah!

Month Five

························•·•·•·•·•·•·························

Psalms 106–121

Psalm 106, Part 1 (Verses 1–24)

This national lament records God's salvation in spite of Israel's rebellion in the desert.

✝ Hallelujah! Give thanks to the gracious LORD, whose mercy endures forever. Who can sing praises to the mighty acts of the LORD? Blest are those who promote justice and always do what is right!

✪ Remember me favorably, O LORD, when you bring salvation to your people, that I may share in the prosperity of your elect, rejoice with them, and find glory in your inheritance.

❖¹ Like our ancestors, we, too, have sinned and acted wickedly. They did not remember your marvelous works in Egypt, nor your abundant love, but rebelled against you at the Red Sea.

● But you saved them in your name, to make your power known.

❖² You rebuked the water at the Red Sea and led them through on dry land. You saved them from those who hated them. The waters covered their oppressors until no one was left.

● You redeemed them from the hand of the enemy.

❖³ Then they believed your words and sang songs of praise to you, their God. But they soon forgot your deeds and did not await your counsel. In the desert, they gave in to their cravings.

● They tested you, O God. So you gave them what they desired.

❖⁴ But you also sent poverty into their soul, so they envied Moses and Aaron, the holy ones of the LORD. The earth opened and swallowed Dathan and engulfed Abiram's followers.

● Fire blazed up in their midst, and flames devoured the wicked.

❖ Israel made a bull-calf at Horeb and worshiped a molten image. They exchanged their Glory for the image of an ox that feeds on grass.

✪ They forgot God their Savior, who had done great and wonderful deeds in Egypt and fearful things at the Red Sea.

✝ You would have destroyed them, but Moses stood before you to turn away your wrath. But still they refused your promised land.

Psalm 106, Part 2 (Verses 25–48)

This national lament recounts how the Israelites continued to sin and follow other gods in the new land. This is the end of Book IV of the Psalms.

✝ The Israelites grumbled in their tents and would not listen to your voice, so you overthrew them in the wilderness and scattered their seed among the nations and throughout the lands.

✿ They united with Baal-Peor and ate sacrifices offered to the dead, thereby provoking your anger, so a plague broke out among them. The plague ended when Phinehas interceded on their behalf. He is remembered to this day as righteous.

❖¹ Israel again provoked your anger at the waters of Meribah, and you punished Moses because he spoke thoughtlessly at the Israelites' response.

● They did not destroy the pagans as you had commanded.

❖² Instead they intermingled with heathens and learned their pagan ways. They sacrificed their sons and their daughters to evil spirits and shed innocent blood to the idols of Canaan.

● They worshiped pagan idols, and it became a trap to them.

❖³ The land was defiled by the blood of their children in Canaan. They were polluted and unfaithful in their actions. Therefore your wrath was kindled against the Israelites.

● You rejected your inheritance and left them to heathen rule.

❖⁴ You gave them over to enemies who oppressed them and humbled them, and they were brought down by their sins.

● Many times you delivered them, but still they rebelled.

❖ You saw their distress and heard their lamentation. You remembered your covenant with them and relented.

✿ In accordance with your great mercy, you caused them to be pitied by their captors. Save us, O LORD our God, and gather us from among the nations, that we may give thanks to your holy name.

✝ Blessed be the LORD, the God of Israel, from everlasting and to everlasting; and let all the people say, "Amen!" Hallelujah!

Psalm 107, Part 1 (Verses 1–22)

Psalm 107 is an individual song of thanksgiving. Throughout history, when people cry out to the LORD, he redeems their life. This begins Book V of the Psalms.

✝ Give thanks for the goodness of the LORD, whose mercy endures forever. Let those whom God redeemed proclaim their salvation.

✿ The LORD gathered them out of the lands, from east and west, from north and south. Some wandered in deserts with no city in which to dwell.

❖¹ They were hungry and thirsty; their spirits were faint within them. When they cried out, the LORD delivered them from their distress.

● You, O LORD, led them safely to a city where they could dwell.

❖² Give thanks to the LORD for the steadfast love and wonderful deeds shown to the children of Israel.

● For you quench their thirst and fill the hungry with good things.

❖³ Some sat in darkness, imprisoned by iron chains, because they had not followed the counsel of the Most High God.

● Their spirits were humbled through labor with no one to help.

❖⁴ They cried out to the LORD and were delivered from their distress. God led them out of darkness and broke their bonds.

● Give thanks to the LORD for the mercy and wonders shown to the faithful.

❖ You shatter the doors of bronze and break the iron bars in two. The foolish who were rebellious were afflicted because of their sins. They couldn't bear to eat food, so they drew near to death.

✿ When they cried out to the LORD in their trouble, they were delivered from their distress. God healed them with a word and saved them from the grave.

✝ Give thanks to the LORD for the unfailing love and wonders shown to the Israelites. Let the redeemed offer a sacrifice of thanksgiving; tell of God's wondrous acts with shouts of joy.

Psalm 107, Part 2 (Verses 22–43)

This individual song of thanksgiving continues to relate how, throughout history, when people cry out to the LORD, he redeems their life.

✝ Let the redeemed tell of God's acts with songs of joy. Merchants who cross the sea in ships, to trade across the waters, have beheld the wondrous works of the LORD in the deep.

✺ When God spoke, a stormy wind arose, which tossed high the seas. The waves rose up to the heavens and fell back to the depths.

❖¹ The sea merchants' hearts melted because of their peril. They swayed and staggered like drunkards and were at their wits' end.

● They cried out to you, O LORD, from their trouble and were delivered.

❖² God stilled the storm and quieted the waves, and they were relieved at the calm sea. God brought them into a safe harbor.

● Give thanks to the LORD for the unfailing love shown to the faithful.

❖³ The LORD turns rivers and springs into deserts and turns fruitful land into salt flats because of the wickedness of the inhabitants.

● We exalt you, God, in the congregation and in the council of elders.

❖⁴ God made pools of water in the deserts and placed springs in dry land. The LORD settled the hungry there to found a city where they could dwell.

● They sowed fields and planted vineyards, and they gathered a fruitful harvest.

❖ You, O LORD, caused both the people and the herds to increase in number.

✺ When they were diminished through stress and sorrow, God showed contempt for princes and made them wander in deserts. But the LORD lifts up the needy and cares for their families like sheep.

✝ The upright will see this and rejoice, while all wickedness will be silenced. Let the wise ponder these things and consider the loving mercies of the LORD.

Psalm 108

This psalm is a national lament by David. (The final seven verses are identical to the final seven verses of Psalm 60.)

✝ My heart is steadfast, O God; I will sing praises from my soul.

✿ Wake up, my spirit; awake, lute and harp. I myself will waken the dawn.

❖¹ I will give you thanks before the nations, O LORD; I will sing your praises among the people. For your steadfast love is greater than the heavens.

● Your faithfulness reaches to the clouds, O LORD.

❖² Exalt yourself above the heavens, O God, and let your glory shine over all the earth, so that those who are dear to you may be delivered.

● O LORD, answer my prayer with the right hand of your salvation.

❖³ God spoke out of the heavens and said, "I will exult and parcel out Shechem; I will divide the valley of Succoth. Gilead and Manasseh are mine.

● Ephraim is my helmet, and Judah is my scepter.

❖⁴ Moab is my washbasin, on Edom I wipe my sandaled feet, and over Philistia will I shout in triumph."

● Who will lead me into the fortified city of Edom?

❖ Have you not rejected us, O God? You no longer go into battle with our armies.

✿ LORD, grant us your help against the enemy, for the help of humans is worthless.

✝ With God we will do valiant deeds, and the LORD shall tread our enemies underfoot.

Psalm 109, Part 1 (Verses 1–16)

This individual lament of David is an imprecatory psalm calling for retribution against an enemy. In it we hear the cry of a broken and hurting person.

✝ Do not remain silent, O God of my praise, for wicked and deceitful mouths are speaking against me with hateful lies.

✪ They speak to me with a lying tongue and attack me without a cause. In return for my love, they accuse me; but still I continue to pray for them.

❖¹ They repay evil for good and hatred for my love. Set a wicked man against the enemy, and let an accuser stand at his right hand.

● O God of my salvation, let my cry come before you.

❖² When he is judged, let him be found guilty and his appeal be in vain. May his days be few, and may another take his position.

● I cry out to you for justice and mercy, O Lord.

❖³ May his children be fatherless waifs and beggars and his wife become a widow. Let them be driven from the ruins of their homes.

● Consider, O Lord, the enemy who has come against me.

❖⁴ Let creditors seize his entire estate and strangers plunder his gains. Let no one show him kindness and no one pity his orphaned children.

● I am persecuted, O Lord; raise your hand to save me.

❖ May his descendants be destroyed and his name blotted out in the next generation. Let the sins of his fathers and mothers be remembered before God.

✪ May their sins be always before you, O Lord, and remove their names from the earth.

✝ For my enemy did not remember to show mercy, but persecuted the poor and needy, and sought to kill the brokenhearted.

Psalm 109, Part 2 (Verses 17–31)

This individual lament of David continues. In his pain, the psalmist calls for retribution against an enemy. We hear the cry of a broken and hurting person.

✝ My accuser loved cursing; may he receive curses. He took no delight in blessing, so he receives no blessing. He made cursing his way of life.

✪ So the curses soaked into his body like water and into his bones like oil; they have become like a cloak or a belt that continually surrounds him.

❖¹ Bring judgment, O Lord, to my accusers and to those who speak evil against me. But you, O my God, deal kindly with me for your name's sake.

● In your tender mercy, O Lord, deliver me from evil.

❖² For I am humbled and in need, and my heart is wounded within me. I am fading away like a shadow at evening; I am shaken off like a locust.

● Hear my cry of desperation when it comes to you, O Lord.

❖³ My knees are weak from fasting, and my flesh is frail and gaunt. I have become an object of scorn; my enemies see me and shake their heads.

● Help me, O Lord my God; save me for your mercy's sake.

❖⁴ Let them know this is your doing, O Lord. They may curse, but you will bring a blessing.

● O Lord my God, do not forget your faithful servant.

❖ Let those who rise up against me be put to shame. Your servant will rejoice when my accusers are clothed with dishonor.

✪ Shame will wrap around them like a cloak. Then I will give great thanks to the Lord with my mouth.

✝ In the midst of the multitude will I praise you, O God, because you stand at the right hand of the needy, to save them from those who would condemn them.

Psalm 110

This royal psalm attributed to David speaks of the coming messiah. Verse 1 is quoted in all three synoptic gospels and in the book of Acts, inferring that David is speaking of the messiah. The first "LORD" translates "YHWH," the proper name of God. The second "Lord" translates "Adonai," which can mean "Lord," "master," or "owner" and can refer to either humans or angels or to God. In this case the second "Lord" represents the coming messiah.

✝ The LORD, Yahweh, said to my Lord, Adonai, "Sit at my right hand."

✿ The LORD said, "Sit in the place of honor at my right hand until I humble your enemies to be your footstool."

   ❖¹ The LORD will send the scepter of your power out from Jerusalem into the midst of your adversaries, saying,

   ● "You will rule over the enemies that surround you."

   ❖² Your loyal subjects gladly follow you to victory, clothed in the sacred garments, as fresh as the morning dew.

   ● In the beauty of holiness have I begotten you.

   ❖³ The LORD has sworn an oath and will not break the vow: "You are to be a priest forever.

   ● You are a priest after the order of Melchizedek."

   ❖⁴ The LORD Most High, who is at your right hand, will smite kings in the day of wrath.

   ● The LORD will extend your rule over all the nations.

   ❖ God will execute justice against the nations, leaving the valleys filled with corpses. God will crush the leaders throughout the whole earth.

✿ Adonai will drink from the brook beside the road, and Yahweh will make him victorious.

✝ The LORD said to my Lord, "You are a priest forever after the order of Melchizedek."

Psalm 111

Psalm 111 is a corporate psalm of praise, extolling the works of God, the words of God, and God's eternal nature. It is an acrostic poem in which the verses begin with consecutive letters of the Hebrew alphabet.

✝ Hallelujah! I will give thanks to the LORD with all my heart, in the assembly of the righteous and in the congregation.

✿ The great and glorious works of our LORD are studied by all who delight in them.

❖¹ Glorious God, your work is full of majesty and splendor, and your righteousness endures forever.

● O LORD, you are gracious and full of compassion.

❖² Your marvelous works, O God, will always be remembered. You provide food to those who call on your name.

● O LORD, you will remember your covenant forever.

❖³ You have shown your people the power of your works by giving them the land that belonged to other nations.

● The works of your hands are faithfulness and justice.

❖⁴ The works of your hands are faithful and just, and all your commandments are trustworthy and sure.

● Your laws stand fast forever and ever, O LORD.

❖ All your works will stand steadfast forever, because they have been performed in truth and faithfulness.

✿ You delivered your people, O LORD, and commanded your covenant to be observed forever. How holy and awesome is your name in all the world!

✝ Reverence for the LORD is the beginning of wisdom; those who act according to God's precepts gain insight and understanding. Let us praise the LORD forever!

Psalm 112

In this wisdom psalm, the ways of the righteous are extolled in contrast to the ways of the wicked mentioned in the last verse. It is an acrostic poem in which the verses begin with consecutive letters of the Hebrew alphabet.

✝ Hallelujah! Praise the LORD! Blessed are all who have reverence for the LORD and take great delight in obeying God's commandments!

☉ Their descendants will be mighty in the land, and their homes will be filled with wealth and riches.

  ❖¹ Light shines in the darkness for the godly; the righteous are merciful and full of compassion.

  ● The generation of the upright will receive blessings.

  ❖² It is good for the godly to be generous in lending and to manage their affairs with justice, for they will never be shaken.

  ● Their righteousness will endure forever.

  ❖³ The righteous will be remembered forever. They will not be afraid of any evil rumors.

  ● Their heart is firmly fixed on trusting the LORD.

  ❖⁴ Their hearts are established in confidence, and they will not be afraid.

  ● The righteous will look triumphantly on their enemies.

  ❖ The godly have given freely to the poor, and their righteousness endures forever. They will hold up their heads with honor.

☉ The wicked will see it and be angry; they will lose heart, and their desires will fade away.

✝ Hallelujah! Blessed are all who fear the LORD and take great delight in obeying God's commands!

Psalm 113

This psalm of praise is constructed around a call to worship and a reason for praise. Here we see a picture of a God who cares for the underdog.

✝ Hallelujah! Give praise, you servants of the LORD; praise the name of the LORD.

✿ Blessed be the name of the LORD, from this time forth forevermore.

❖¹ From the rising of the sun to its setting, let the name of the LORD be praised all day.

● Praise the name of the LORD from the east to the west.

❖² The LORD is exalted above all nations and God's splendor above the heavens.

● The glory of the LORD extends to all creation.

❖³ Who is like the LORD our God, who sits enthroned on high but bends down to behold all creation in the skies and on the earth?

● The LORD descends to behold the heavens and the earth.

❖⁴ God picks up the weak from the dust of the ground and lifts up the poor from the garbage heap.

● God will raise the weak and the poor out of the dusty earth.

❖ The LORD seats them among the nobility, with the princes of the holy people.

✿ God makes the woman who dwells in a childless house to become a joyful mother of children. Hallelujah!

✝ Give praise, you servants of the LORD; praise the name of the LORD. Hallelujah! Praise the LORD!

Psalm 114

This psalm of praise extolls God for his mighty deeds during the journey from Egypt to the promised land.

✝ Hallelujah! When Israel came out of Egypt and the house of Jacob withdrew from a people of foreign speech,

✪ Then Judah became God's sanctuary, and Israel became the dominion of the LORD.

❖ 1 The Red Sea beheld their coming and fled; Jordan turned and went back.

● The waters took notice of the glory of God.

❖ 2 The mountains skipped like rams and the little hills like young sheep.

● All the earth rejoices at the wonders of the LORD.

❖ 3 What ailed you, O sea, that you fled? O Jordan, why did you turn back?

● The waters fled at the presence of the God of Jacob.

❖ 4 You mountains, why did you skip like rams? You little hills, why did you shake like young sheep?

● The earth trembled in the presence of the LORD.

❖ Tremble, O earth, in the presence of the LORD your God, who is the God of Jacob.

✪ This is the God who turned hard rock into pools of water and caused a flowing spring to appear in flint stone.

✝ Hallelujah! When Israel came out of Egypt, then Judah became God's sanctuary.

Psalm 115

This national psalm of confidence records God's actions when, even after their entry into the promised land, the Israelites continued to rebel.

✝ Not to us, O LORD, but to your name give glory, because of your unfailing love and your faithfulness.

☉ Why should heathens say, "Where then is their God?" O God, you are in your heaven, and you do whatever pleases you.

❖¹ Their idols are made of silver and gold, fashioned by human hands. They have mouths but cannot speak, and eyes but do not see. They have ears that do not hear and noses that do not smell.

● They are merely idols crafted by human hands.

❖² They have hands but cannot feel, and feet that do not walk; they make no sound. Those who craft them and those who trust them are like the idols themselves, without sense or knowledge.

● O Israel, trust in the LORD our God, who is our help and shield.

❖³ O house of Aaron, trust in the LORD, who is your help and shield. All you who fear the LORD, trust in our God, who is your help and shield.

● All who revere the LORD, both great and small, will be blessed.

❖⁴ The LORD has been mindful of us and will bless us; God will bless both the houses of Israel and of Aaron. May the LORD continue to bless you and the generations to come.

● May the LORD, maker of heaven and earth, bless you and keep you.

❖ Heaven is the LORD's domain, but the earth has been entrusted to all humanity.

☉ The dead do not sing praise to the LORD, nor do those who have gone down into the silence of the grave.

✝ But we will bless the LORD and sing praises from now until forever. Hallelujah!

Psalm 116

Psalm 116 is an individual psalm of thanksgiving for what God has done in the past or will do in the future. Only two psalms express love of the LORD, this one and Psalm 18.

✝ I love the LORD because God has heard the voice of my supplication; the LORD listens to me whenever I call.

✪ Deadly cords entangled me, the grip of the grave drew me in, and I was overcome by grief and sorrow. Then I called upon the name of the LORD: "I pray to you, O LORD, preserve my life."

❖¹ The LORD watches over the innocent; when I was in serious trouble, God delivered me. You may rest once again, O my soul, for the LORD has treated you well.

● Our gracious and righteous LORD is full of compassion.

❖² You rescued my life from death, my eyes from tears, and my feet from stumbling. I will walk in the presence of the LORD.

● I will serve the LORD in the land of the living.

❖³ I believed even when I spoke of my affliction. In my distress I cried out, "These people are liars!" How can I repay the LORD for all the blessings poured out on me?

● I will raise the cup of salvation and call on God's holy name.

❖⁴ I will fulfill my vows to the LORD in the presence of all people. God cares deeply when any of his faithful followers die. Precious in your sight, O LORD, is the death of your servants.

● I will offer a sacrifice of thanksgiving and call upon your name.

❖ O LORD, I am your servant and the child of your handmaid; you have unshackled me and set me free.

✪ I will fulfill my vows to the LORD in the presence of all the faithful.

✝ I will fulfill my vows in the courts of God's house, in your midst, O Jerusalem. Hallelujah!

Psalm 100 and Psalm 117

No author is identified for either of these psalms. Both are psalms of praise and joy in the LORD, and both are a call to worship. This prayer begins with Psalm 100; as you leave the circle on the repeat of cruciform 1, the last three beads are from Psalm 117.

✝ Be joyful in the LORD, all you lands, and serve the LORD with gladness.

⊙ Serve the LORD with gladness and come into God's presence with a song of joy.

❖ ¹ Know this: Yahweh is the God who made us, and we belong to the LORD.

● We are God's people, the sheep who graze in green pastures.

❖ ² Enter the gates with thanksgiving; go into God's courts with a song of praise.

● Give thanks to the LORD and call upon God's holy name.

❖ ³ For the LORD is good. This is our God, whose steadfast love endures forever.

● God's faithfulness continues to every generation.

❖ ⁴ Make a joyful noise to the LORD, all the earth; worship our God with great gladness.

● Come into God's presence with a song of joy.

❖ Sing praise to the LORD, the whole earth; worship our God, all you peoples.

⊙ Great is God's steadfast love toward us, for the faithfulness of our LORD endures forever.

✝ Hallelujah! Praise the LORD, all you nations.

Psalm 118, Part 1 (Verses 1–16)

This psalm is a national psalm of thanksgiving. It was most likely sung by a cantor with congregational responses, so you will notice a large number of repetitions.

✝ We give thanks to you, O LORD, for you are good and your mercy endures forever.

☉ Let Israel and the house of Aaron now proclaim, "God's mercy endures forever."

❖¹ Let those who fear the LORD now proclaim, "God's mercy endures forever." Out of distress, I called out to the LORD; the LORD answered by setting me free. I will not fear.

● With the LORD at my side, what can mortals do to me?

❖² The LORD is at my side to help me; I will triumph over those who hate me. It is better to rely on the LORD than to put any trust in rulers.

● It is better to rely on the LORD than to put any trust in mortals.

❖³ All the ungodly surround me; in the name of the LORD I will repel them. They encircle me; they hem me in on every side.

● In the name of the LORD I will cut them off.

❖⁴ The ungodly swarmed about me like bees but were extinguished by the blaze of fire from the thorn bushes.

● In the name of the LORD I will cut them off.

❖ They attacked me so viciously that I almost perished, but the LORD came to my help. The LORD is my strength and my song, and he has become my salvation.

☉ Shouts of joy and victory resound in the tents of the righteous of the LORD. "The right hand of the LORD has triumphed!

✝ The right hand of the LORD is exalted! The right hand of the LORD has triumphed!"

Psalm 118, Part 2 (Verses 15–29)

This national psalm of thanksgiving continues. It is messianic in nature, a call to welcome the coming messiah.

✝ There is a sound of exultation and victory in the tents of the righteous. "The right hand of the LORD has triumphed!

✿ The right hand of the LORD is exalted! The right hand of the LORD has triumphed!"

❖¹ The LORD punished me severely but did not hand me over to death. Open for me the gates of righteousness; I will enter them and offer thanks to you, O LORD.

● I shall not die but live to declare the works of the LORD.

❖² This is the gate of the LORD; only the righteous may enter. I will give thanks to you, O LORD.

● For you answered me and have become my salvation.

❖³ The same stone that the builders rejected has become the chief cornerstone. This is the LORD's doing, and it is marvelous in our sight.

● This is the day the LORD has made; we will rejoice and be glad in it.

❖⁴ Save us, O LORD, deliver us! We beseech you, O LORD, to grant us success. Blessed is the one who comes in the name of Yahweh.

● We bow down to you in the temple of the LORD.

❖ The LORD our God has shined upon us. Join in the pilgrim procession and take leafy boughs to bind up the vestal sacrifice to the horns of the altar.

✿ You are my God, and I will give you thanks; you are my God, and I will exalt you.

✝ We give thanks to you, O LORD, for you are good, and your mercy endures forever.

Psalm 119, Part 1 (Verses 1–16)

Psalm 119 is a wisdom psalm and is the longest psalm in the Bible. It is also an acrostic poem made up of sets of verses; each set is assigned to a letter of the Hebrew alphabet. In each set, all eight verses begin with the same letter. Each prayer will cover sixteen verses. We begin with א (*aleph*) and ב (*bet*).

✝ Blessed are those whose way is blameless, who walk in the law of the LORD! Blessed are they who observe God's decrees.

✪ Blessed are they who seek God with all their hearts, who never do any wrong, but always walk in the way of the LORD.

❖¹ You laid down your commandments, that we should fully keep them. Establish my ways, O LORD, that I may consistently keep your statutes. Then I shall not be put to shame.

● For my eyes will be fixed on all your commandments.

❖² I will thank you with a sincere heart, when I have learned your righteous judgments.

● I will obey your statutes; do not utterly abandon me.

❖³ How will young persons remain pure? By keeping to your words and seeking you with their whole heart.

● Do not let me stray from your commandments, O LORD.

❖⁴ I treasure your promise in my heart, so that I might not sin against you. I have recited aloud all the judgments of your mouth.

● Blessed are you, O LORD; teach me all your statutes.

❖ I have taken greater delight in the way of your decrees than in all manner of riches.

✪ I will meditate on your commandments and reflect on your ways.

✝ I take delight in all your statutes; I will not forget your word.

Psalm 119, Part 2 (Verses 17–32)

This wisdom psalm emphasizes the traditional teachings from Israel's wise men. Wisdom psalms often contain meditations on the goodness of the law. Here are ג (*gimel*) and ד (*dalet*).

✝ Deal bountifully with your servant, that I may live and keep your word.

☉ Open my eyes, that I may behold the wonders of your law. I am a sojourner here on earth; do not hide your commandments from me.

❖¹ You have rebuked the arrogant; those who stray from your commandments find themselves under a curse.

● My soul is consumed at all times with longing for your justice.

❖² Spare me shame and rebuke, for I have kept your decrees. Even though rulers sit and plot against me, I will still meditate on your statutes.

● For your decrees are my delight and my companions.

❖³ My soul clings to the dust; give me life according to your word. When I had confessed my ways, you answered me.

● Instruct me in your statutes, O Lord.

❖⁴ Help me understand the meaning of your commandments, so that I may meditate on your marvelous works. My soul is weary from sorrow.

● Strengthen me, O Lord, according to your word.

❖ Help me not to give in to deceitful temptation, but let me find grace through your law; for I have chosen the way of faithfulness.

☉ I have set your justice before me, and I hold fast to your decrees. O Lord, let me never be put to shame.

✝ I will follow the way of your commandments, for you have set my heart free.

Psalm 119, Part 3 (Verses 33–48)

Wisdom psalms often point out the necessity of practicing righteousness. Here are ה (*he*) and ו (*vav*).

✝ Teach me, O LORD, the way of your statutes, and I will keep it to the end.

✿ Give me understanding, so I may obey your law; I will keep it with all my heart. Lead me in the path of your commandments, for that is my desire.

  ❖¹ Turn my heart toward your decrees and not to unjust gains. Turn my eyes from watching vain promises.

  ● Restore my life to your mission, O LORD.

  ❖² Fulfill your promise to your servant, O LORD, which will produce reverence for you. Take away the disgrace that I dread, because your judgments are beneficial.

  ● I long for your commandments. LORD, preserve my life in righteousness.

  ❖³ Let your loving kindness come to me, O LORD, with your promised salvation.

  ● Because I trust in your words, I will have a reply for those who taunt me.

  ❖⁴ Do not take your word of truth out of my mouth, for my hope resides in your ordinances. I will continue to keep your law forever.

  ● I will walk in liberty, because I follow your decrees.

  ❖ I will testify to your merits before kings and will not be ashamed.

✿ For I delight in your commandments, which I have always loved.

✝ Then I will lift up my hands and meditate on your statutes.

Psalm 119, Part 4 (Verses 49–64)

Wisdom psalms sometimes contrast the ways of the righteous with the ways of the arrogant or wicked. Here are ז (*zayin*) and ח (*khet*).

✝ Remember your word to your servant, because you have given me hope.

❂ In my distress, my comfort lies in your promise that gives me life. Even though the arrogant mock me cruelly, still I have not turned away from your law.

❖¹ I find great comfort when I remember your judgments of old. But I am filled with burning rage when I see the wicked forsake your law.

● Your statutes have been like songs to me, O Lord.

❖² Your statutes have been like songs to me wherever I have lived in a strange land. I remember your name in the night, O Lord, and dwell on your law.

● My practice, O Lord, has been to obey your commandments.

❖³ You only are my portion, O Lord; I promise to keep your words. I entreat you with all my heart,

● Be merciful to me according to your promise.

❖⁴ When I considered my ways, O Lord, I turned my feet toward your decrees.

● I hasten without delay to keep your commandments.

❖ Though the cords of the wicked surround me, I do not forget your law. At midnight I will rise to praise you for your righteous plans.

❂ I am a companion of all who revere you and of those committed to following your rules.

✝ The earth, O Lord, is filled with your love; teach me your statutes.

Psalm 119, Part 5 (Verses 65–80)

Wisdom psalms sometimes acknowledge one's own need to be disciplined by the LORD. Here are ט (*tet*) and י (*yod*).

✝ You have dealt graciously with your servant, O LORD, according to your word.

✿ Teach me discernment and knowledge, for I have believed in your commandments. Before I was humbled I went astray, but now I keep your word.

❖¹ You are good and you bring forth good; teach me your statutes. The arrogant have smeared me with lies.

● But I will keep your commandments with my whole heart.

❖² Their hearts are calloused, but my delight is in your law. It is good for me that I have been humbled, so that I might learn your statutes.

● The law you have spoken is more precious than gold and silver.

❖³ Your hands have molded and fashioned me; give me understanding, so I may learn your commandments. Those who follow you will be glad when they see me.

● For I have put my trust in your word, O LORD.

❖⁴ I know, O LORD, that your judgments are right and that in faithfulness you have humbled me.

● According to your promise, O LORD, let your loving kindness be my comfort.

❖ Let your compassion come to me, that I may live, for your law is my delight. Let the arrogant be put to shame for wronging me without cause.

✿ But I will meditate on your commandments. Let me unite with those who revere you and with those who know your decrees.

✝ Let my heart be fully committed to your statutes, O LORD, that I may not be put to shame.

Psalm 119, Part 6 (Verses 81–96)

Wisdom psalms may acknowledge a hope that abides even in the face of disappointment. Here are ‏כ‎ (*kaph*) and ‏ל‎ (*lamed*).

✝ My soul longs for your salvation; I have put all my hope in your word.

✿ My eyes long to see your promise fulfilled, and I wonder when you will comfort me. Though I am shriveled like a wineskin in the smoke, still I have not forgotten your statutes.

❖¹ How much longer must I wait? When will you judge those who persecute me? The arrogant, who do not follow your law, have dug pits to trap me. Protect me from their lies, O Lord.

● Help me, for all your commandments are faithful.

❖² They have almost wiped me from the earth, but I will not forsake your covenant.

● In your steadfast love, revive me so I may obey your decrees, O Lord.

❖³ O Lord, your eternal word stands firmly fixed in the heavens. Then you established the earth to endure.

● Your faithfulness extends to every generation.

❖⁴ By your decree they continue to stand even to this day, for all created things long to serve you. I might have perished in my sorrow.

● But my delight in your law sustains me, O Lord.

❖ I will never forget your commandments, O Lord, for by them you have given me life.

✿ I belong to you, O Lord, and I have sought your commands. Rescue me, for I know the wicked lie in wait to destroy me.

✝ I will diligently observe your decrees, for I have seen that even though perfection has a limit, your commandment has no bounds.

Psalm 119, Part 7 (Verses 97–112)

Wisdom psalms stress the necessity of practicing righteousness. Here are מ (*mem*) and נ (*nun*).

✝ Oh, how I love your law! All the day long I ponder the wonder of it.

✡ Your commandments are my constant guide, for they make me wiser than my enemies. I have more insight than all my teachers, for I meditate on your decrees.

❖ [1] I am even wiser than the elders, because I observe your precepts. I will follow your instructions.

● I will restrain my feet from every evil path.

❖ [2] I do not shrink from your ordinances, because you yourself have taught me. How sweet are your words to my taste!

● Your words are sweeter than honey to my mouth.

❖ [3] Through your precepts I gain understanding; therefore I hate every lying way.

● Your word is a lantern to my feet and a light upon my path.

❖ [4] I have sworn a solemn vow to keep your righteous judgments. I have already suffered much.

● Preserve my life, O Lord, according to your word.

❖ Accept, O Lord, the willing tribute of my lips and teach me your judgments. My life is a continual struggle, yet I do not forget your law.

✡ Although the wicked have set a trap for me, I have not strayed from your commandments. Your testimonies are my inheritance forever; truly, they are the joy of my heart.

✝ I have applied my heart to the fulfillment of your statutes forever and to the very end.

Psalm 119, Part 8 (Verses 113–128)

A wisdom psalm may bargain with God for protection against arrogant oppressors. Here are ס (*samek*) and ע (*ayin*).

✝ I despise those who have divided loyalties because I love your law.

✿ You are my hiding place and my shield; all my hope is found in your word. Let the wicked depart from me, so that I may keep the commandments of my God.

  ❖¹ Sustain me according to your promise, so that I may live and not be disappointed.

  ● Sustain me safely in hope, so that my delight will always be in your statutes.

  ❖² You spurn all who stray from your ordinances; their deceitfulness is in vain. In your sight, all the wicked of the earth are cast off like dross.

  ● But I love your decrees and stand in awe of your judgments.

  ❖³ My flesh trembles in awe of you. I have done what is just and right, O Lord; do not deliver me to my oppressors.

  ● Guarantee your servant's well-being and save me from the arrogant.

  ❖⁴ My eyes long to see your salvation and your righteous promise. Teach me your statutes, O Lord.

  ● Deal with your servant according to your loving kindness.

  ❖ I am your servant; grant me understanding, so I may understand your testimony. It is time for you to act, O Lord, against those who have broken your law.

✿ Truly, I love your commandments, O Lord, much more than fine gold or precious gems.

✝ I hold all your commandments to be right for me, and I abhor all paths that lead to deception.

Psalm 119, Part 9 (Verses 129–144)

Following the path of faith in God can be difficult. Wisdom psalms often give perspective and balance to the struggle. Here are פ (*pe*) and צ (*tsade*).

✝ Your decrees are wonderful, O Lord; therefore I will obey them with all my heart and soul.

✿ When your word goes forth, it gives light and understanding to the simple. I open my mouth and pant with expectation as I long for your commandments.

❖¹ Turn to me in mercy, as you always do to those who love your name. Guide my footsteps in your word and let no vanity gain control over me.

● Rescue me from those who oppress me, O Lord.

❖² Tears stream from my eyes when people disobey your law. Teach me your statutes, and I will keep your commandments.

● Let your countenance shine upon your servant.

❖³ You are righteous, O Lord, and upright in your judgments. Therefore my indignation consumes me when my adversaries forget your words.

● For you issue your decrees with justice and in perfect faithfulness.

❖⁴ Your word has been thoroughly tested, and your servant holds it dear. I am small and insignificant.

● But I do not forget your commandments, O Lord.

❖ Your righteousness provides an everlasting justice, and your law is enduring truth.

✿ Trouble and distress have come upon me, yet your commandments remain my delight.

✝ The righteousness of your decrees is eternal; grant me insight, that I may live.

Psalm 119, Part 10 (Verses 145–160)

Wisdom psalms emphasize the traditional teachings of the wise leaders of Israel. Here are ק (*qoph*) and ר (*resh*).

✝ I cry out with my whole heart; answer me, O LORD, that I may keep your statutes.

✿ Save me, O LORD, and I will keep your decrees. I arise before dawn and cry out in the early morning, for I put my trust in your word.

❖¹ My eyes are open through the night watches, so I may meditate on your promise. Hear my voice, O LORD, in accordance with your steadfast love.

● According to your judgments, preserve my life.

❖² The enemy draws near in malicious pursuit; they are very far from your law. Yet you, O LORD, are near at hand, and all your commandments are true.

● I have long known that your decrees will last forever.

❖³ Behold my misery and deliver me, for I do not forget your law. Plead my cause and redeem me.

● O LORD, give me life according to your promise.

❖⁴ Deliverance is far from the wicked, for they do not seek your statutes. Great is your compassion, O LORD.

● Preserve my life, according to your standard.

❖ There are many who persecute and oppress me, yet I have not swerved from your decrees. I look with loathing at the faithless who have abandoned your word.

✿ Consider how I love your commandments! Revive me, O LORD, in your loving kindness.

✝ The heart of your word is truth, and all your righteous judgments endure for eternity.

Psalm 119, Part 11 (Verses 161–176)

Although this wisdom psalm often talks about the necessity of following the law and meditating on the law, it never defines what that law says. It only emphasizes that it is to be revered. Here are שׁ (*shin/sin*) and ת (*tav*).

✝ Rulers may persecute me without a cause, but my heart stands in awe of your words.

✪ I am as glad because of your promise as another is who finds great treasure. I hate all manner of deceitful lies, but your law is my delight.

❖¹ Seven times a day I praise you for your righteous judgments. There is great peace for those who love your law; nothing will cause them to stumble.

● I place my hope in your salvation, O LORD.

❖² I have fulfilled your commandments and kept your decrees, because I have loved them deeply.

● I keep your decrees, O LORD, for you know all my ways.

❖³ Let my cry come before you, O LORD; give me understanding according to your word. Hear my supplication and deliver me, according to your promise.

● My lips will sing your praise when you teach me your laws.

❖⁴ My tongue will sing of your promise, for I know all your commandments are righteous. Let your hand be ready to help me.

● For I choose to obey all your commandments, O LORD.

❖ I long for your salvation, O LORD, and I find great delight in your law.

✪ Let me live, and my soul will ever praise you. I look for your ordinances to sustain me.

✝ I have gone astray like a sheep that is lost; search for your servant, for I do not forget your commandments.

Psalm 120

This individual lament was used as a song of ascents to be sung while going to the temple for Passover, Pentecost, or the Feast of Tabernacles.

✝ In my day of trouble, I cried out to the LORD; I called to the LORD my God, who answered me.

✪ Deliver my soul, O LORD, from lying lips and from deceitful tongues.

❖¹ What shall be done to those who have deceit on their lips? And what more will be done to the deceitful tongue?

● Deliver me, O LORD, when I cry out to you.

❖² The deceitful will be pierced by the sharpened arrows of a warrior and burned with hot glowing coals from a broom tree.

● Preserve my life, O LORD, when I am among the enemy.

❖³ Alas, how I hate being a sojourner in the land of Meshech and dwelling among the tents of Kedar!

● Remain with me, O LORD, when I face my foes.

❖⁴ Too long have I had to live among the enemies of peace.

● Bring me out, O LORD, to a place among the faithful.

❖ I am on the side of peace; but whenever I speak of it, they want to wage war.

✪ Deliver my soul, O LORD, from lying lips and from deceitful tongues.

✝ In my day of trouble, I cried out to the LORD; I called to the LORD my God, who answered me.

Psalm 121

Psalm 121 is a song of ascents and an individual psalm of confidence. The pilgrims are headed up to the mountain of the LORD, and they know that he is the source of their help.

✝ I lift up my eyes to the hills. From where does my help come?

✪ My help comes from the LORD, the maker of heaven and earth.

❖¹ O LORD, you will not let our foot be moved, and you who watch over us will not fall asleep.

● The LORD will not allow your foot to stumble or slip.

❖² Behold, the one who watches over Israel shall neither slumber nor sleep.

● The LORD who watches over you will not fall asleep.

❖³ The LORD alone watches over you; the LORD is your shade at your right hand.

● The LORD, who is your keeper, watches over you.

❖⁴ The sun will not strike you by day, nor the moon by night.

● The LORD will shade you from both the sun and the moon.

❖ The LORD will protect you from all evil; it is our LORD who will keep you safe.

✪ The LORD shall watch over your going out and your coming in, from this time forth and forevermore.

✝ I lift up my eyes to the hills. My help comes from the maker of heaven and earth.

Month Six

• • • • •

Psalms 122–150

Psalm 122

This psalm is a song of Zion attributed to David and used as a song of ascents. These songs were sung by pilgrims on their way to Jerusalem for one of the annual feasts.

✝ I was glad when they said to me, "Let us go to the house of the LORD."

☉ Now our feet are standing within your gates, O Jerusalem.

❖¹ Jerusalem is built as a city that is united together, a city to which all the tribes go up.

● The tribes go up to praise the name of the LORD.

❖² For there stand the thrones of judgment, the thrones of the house of David.

● The assembly of Israel goes up to hear the decrees.

❖³ Pray for the peace of Jerusalem: "May those who love you prosper."

● May the name of the LORD be praised forever.

❖⁴ May peace be within your walls, a time of quietness and tranquility within your towers.

● May the tribes find peace within your walls, O Jerusalem.

❖ For the sake of my family and friends, I pray for your peace and welfare.

☉ For the sake of the dwelling of the LORD our God, I will seek your prosperity.

✝ I was glad when they said to me, "Let us go to the house of the LORD."

Psalm 123

Psalm 123 is a national lament, also used as a song of ascents. Although they are mocked by the scoffers, the faithful move toward Jerusalem and their LORD. As the eyes of a servant are fixed on their master, so should our eyes be fixed on our LORD.

✝ To you, O LORD, I lift up my eyes.

✿ For you alone, O LORD, are enthroned in the heavens.

❖¹ As the eyes of servants look to the hand of their masters,

● So my eyes look to you, O LORD, my God.

❖² And as the eyes of a maid look to the hand of her mistress,

● So will I look to you, O my God.

❖³ And so our eyes look toward the LORD our God, who shows us mercy.

● The LORD our God is always gracious to us.

❖⁴ Because we have endured enough contempt and humiliation,

● Have mercy upon us, O LORD, have mercy.

❖ We have seen contempt from the scorn of the indolent rich.

✿ We have seen contempt from the ridicule of the proud and haughty.

✝ To you, O LORD, I lift up my eyes, to you who are enthroned in heaven.

Psalm 124

This national song of thanksgiving attributed to David is also used as a song of ascents. It is an affirmation that the LORD is faithful to protect and shield believers.

✝ Our help is in the name of the LORD, the maker of heaven and earth.

⊙ If the LORD had not been on our side, let Israel now say—

❖¹ If the LORD had not been on our side, when enemies rose up to attack us—

● Our help is in the name of the LORD.

❖² If the LORD had not been on our side, then our enemies would have swallowed us up alive in their fierce anger toward us.

● Blessed be the LORD, who is on our side.

❖³ Then the floodwaters would have engulfed us and the torrent swept away our soul.

● Our help comes from the maker of heaven and earth.

❖⁴ Then the fury of the raging waters would have swept right over us.

● Blessed be the LORD, who rescues us.

❖ Blessed be the LORD our God, for you did not hand us over as if we were prey for their teeth.

⊙ We have escaped like a bird from the snare of the fowler; the snare is broken, and we have been set free.

✝ Our help is in the name of the LORD, creator of the heavens and the earth.

Psalm 125

Psalm 125 is a song of ascents, a national psalm of confidence that the LORD will not allow the wicked to lead the righteous astray.

✝ The righteous who trust in the LORD are like Mount Zion, which cannot be moved.

⊙ Those who trust in the LORD are like Mount Zion, which will stand secure forever.

❖¹ The hills stand about Jerusalem; so does the LORD stand round about the faithful in the land from this time forth.

● O LORD, stand among your faithful people forever.

❖² The scepter of the wicked will not be permitted to rule over the land allotted to the just.

● O LORD, surround the faithful and keep them secure.

❖³ The righteous who live in the land will not be tempted to put their hands to evil ways.

● Those who trust in the LORD will stand fast forever.

❖⁴ Show your goodness, O LORD, to those who are good.

● Show your goodness to those who are true of heart.

❖ As for those who turn aside to crooked ways, the LORD will lead them away with the evildoers.

⊙ The LORD will lead away the evildoers, so that Israel may experience peace in their land.

✝ Those who trust in the LORD are like Mount Zion, which cannot be moved and stands fast forever.

Psalm 126

This psalm is a national lament that serves as a song of ascents. This psalm expresses the joy felt by the captives in Babylon when they learned that King Cyrus would allow them to go back home.

✝ When the LORD restored the fortunes of Zion, then were we like those who dream.

✪ When the LORD brought back the captives to Zion, then were our mouths filled with laughter.

❖ ¹ Then our tongues were filled with shouts of joy, and it was said among the nations,

● "The LORD has done great things for them."

❖ ² When the LORD brought back the captives to Zion, we were filled with great joy.

● Our God has accomplished amazing things for us.

❖ ³ Restore our fortunes, O LORD, like streams of water in the Negev desert.

● Restore our fortunes, O LORD our God.

❖ ⁴ Those who sowed with tears will reap with songs of joy.

● Give us songs of joy to replace our tears, O LORD.

❖ Those who go out weeping, who are carrying the seed, will return with songs of joy, shouldering their harvest sheaves.

✪ The LORD will restore the fortunes of Zion and fill our mouths with laughter.

✝ The LORD will turn our tears of weeping into songs of joy at our return.

Psalm 127

This wisdom psalm attributed to Solomon was used as a song of ascents. The city of Zion has natural protections, but, more importantly, it is protected by the LORD. Our human efforts are worth little if the LORD does not bless our endeavors.

✝ Unless the LORD builds the house, those who build it labor in vain.

✪ Unless the LORD keeps watch over the city, the watchman stays awake watching in vain.

   ❖¹ It is vain that you rise so early and go to bed so late.

   ● For God alone gives rest to beloved followers.

   ❖² It is also vain to eat the bread gained through toil.

   ● For God gives the beloved rest from their labors.

   ❖³ Children are a gift and a heritage from the LORD.

   ● Yes, the fruit of the womb is a gift from God.

   ❖⁴ Like arrows in the hand of a warrior are the children of one's youth.

   ● God blesses the children born in our home.

   ❖ Happy are those who have a quiver full of them!

✪ Blessed are those who are not put to shame when they contend with their enemies at the city gate.

✝ Unless the LORD builds the house, those who build it labor in vain.

Psalm 128

This wisdom psalm was used as a song of ascents. This psalm begins by declaring a blessing on everyone who stands in awe of God. The same word is used for awe, fear, or reverence. But the psalm also moves to focus on a man who is a husband and father.

✝ Blessed is everyone who has reverence for the LORD!

☉ Blessed are they who follow in the ways of the LORD.

❖¹ You shall eat the fruit that your labor has produced.

● Happiness and prosperity will be yours.

❖² Your wife will be like a fruitful vine flourishing within your house.

● For God brings forth children for the faithful.

❖³ Your children will be like olive shoots springing up around your table.

● The LORD will bless you out of Zion.

❖⁴ The believer who has reverence for the LORD will indeed be blessed.

● May you see the prosperity of Jerusalem.

❖ The LORD bless you from Zion; may you see the prosperity of Jerusalem all the days of your life.

☉ May you live to see your children's children, the generations to come; and may peace reign upon all of Israel.

✝ Blessed are all who revere our God and who follow the way of the LORD!

Psalm 129

This national psalm of confidence was used as a song of ascents. The opposition Israel has suffered throughout its history is personified in this psalm. Regardless, confidence in God's ability to save shows through.

✝ Let Israel now say, "Greatly have they oppressed me since my youth.

✪ Greatly have my enemies persecuted me, but they have not prevailed against me.

❖¹ The plowmen plowed upon my back and made their furrows long."

● My back was covered with the scars of my oppression.

❖² The LORD, the Righteous One, has freed me from the cords of the wicked.

● Our LORD has rescued me from the evil ones.

❖³ Let all those who are enemies of Zion be thrown back in shame.

● O LORD, raise your hand to save us.

❖⁴ Let our enemies be like grass upon the housetops, which withers before it can be plucked.

● Watch over me, O LORD; save me from my enemies.

❖ The grass will not fill the hand of the reaper nor the arms of those who bind the sheaves.

✪ Let those who pass by my enemy not say, "The LORD prosper you. We wish you well in the name of the LORD."

✝ Greatly have they oppressed me since my youth, but the LORD has freed me from the evil ones.

Psalm 130

Psalm 130 is an individual lament attributed to David and used as a psalm of ascents. The beginning focus is on individual sin, but it moves to include forgiveness for all who are penitent.

✝ Out of the depths of despair have I called to you, O LORD.

☉ LORD, hear my cry; let your ears consider well the voice of my supplication.

❖ If you were to keep a record of our sins, O LORD, who could stand?

● LORD, you look to our faith rather than our sins.

❖² For you are always willing to offer forgiveness; therefore we stand in awe of you.

● With you, O LORD, there is forgiveness of sins.

❖³ I wait for the LORD; body and soul, my whole being waits for the LORD.

● I place all my trust in your holy word, O LORD.

❖⁴ My soul waits for the LORD, more than watchmen for the morning.

● My soul waits like watchmen who long to see the dawn.

❖ O Israel, wait for the LORD, for with the LORD there is mercy.

☉ With God there is abundant redemption, and Israel will be redeemed from all their sins.

✝ I wait for the LORD, body and soul; all my hope rests on the word of my God.

Psalm 131 and Psalm 134

Psalm 131 (only three verses long) is an individual psalm of confidence by David. Psalm 134 (only two verses long) is a song of Zion. Both psalms were used as songs of ascents for the faithful people traveling to Jerusalem on their pilgrimage.

✝ Lord, my heart is not proud, and my eyes are not haughty.

✪ O Lord, I do not occupy myself with matters too great for me.

  ❖¹ I do not occupy myself with things that are too difficult for me.

  ● I have learned to still my soul and quiet my mind.

  ❖² I quiet my mind like a child upon his mother's breast.

  ● Like a child, my soul is quiet within me.

  ❖³ From this time forth and forevermore,

  ● O Israel, put your trust in the Lord.

  ❖⁴ Behold now, bless the Lord, all you servants of the Lord.

  ● Lift up your hands in the sanctuary and bless the Lord.

  ❖ You who stand by night in the house of the Lord, bless the Lord.

✪ May the Lord who made heaven and earth bless you out of Zion.

✝ O Israel, wait upon the Lord, from this time forth forevermore.

Psalm 132

This royal psalm was used as a song of ascents. The psalmist cries out of his own despair. Cruciform 1 (verse 6) may refer to the ark of the covenant or simply be the call to a place of worship.

✝ Lord, remember David and all the hardships he endured, how he swore an oath and made a vow to the Mighty One of Jacob.

✪ "I will not enter my house nor lie on my bed; I will not sleep or slumber until I find a dwelling place for God, the Mighty One of Jacob."

❖¹ We heard it was in Ephrathah, but we found it in the fields of Jaar. Let us go to the Lord's dwelling place and worship at God's footstool.

● With the ark of your strength, arise, O Lord, and enter into your resting place.

❖² May your priests be clothed with righteousness and your faithful people sing with joy. For the sake of your servant David, do not reject your anointed one.

● The Lord has sworn an oath to David and will not break it:

❖³ "A son, the fruit of your body, will sit on your throne. If your children keep my covenant and listen to my teaching, their children will also sit upon your throne forevermore.

● For I, the Lord, have chosen Zion as my desired habitation.

❖⁴ This shall be my resting place, and here I will dwell forever, for Zion is my delight.

● I will bless her abundantly, and satisfy her poor with bread.

❖ I will clothe her priests with salvation, and her faithful people will rejoice and sing.

✪ There will I make the horn of David flourish; for I have prepared a lamp for my anointed.

✝ I will clothe his enemies with shame, but my anointed will wear a shining crown."

Psalm 133

This wisdom psalm attributed to David was used as a psalm of ascents. This psalm affirms unity as a quality to be desired.

✝ Oh, how good and pleasant it is when brethren live together in unity!

✱ When families live together in harmony, it is like precious oil poured upon the head.

❖¹ It is like fine oil upon the head that runs down and into the beard.

● It is like fragrant oil poured over the head.

❖² It runs down into the beard of Aaron and down upon the collar of his robe.

● Precious oil of blessing permeates the anointed.

❖³ The oil upon the head is like the dew of Mount Hermon.

● Dew falls upon the mountains of the Lord in blessing.

❖⁴ It is like the dew that falls upon the hills of Zion.

● God bestows a blessing from holy Zion.

❖ For there the Lord has ordained the blessing for those living in harmony; they will have life forevermore.

✱ Oh, how good and pleasant it is when families live together in unity!

✝ For the Lord has commanded the blessing; they shall have life forevermore.

Psalm 131 and Psalm 134

Psalm 131 is an individual psalm of confidence attributed to David. Psalm 134 (beginning at cruciform 4) is a song of Zion. Both psalms were used as songs of ascents. Psalm 134 speaks of those priests and Levites who continue to offer praise in the temple on behalf of the pilgrims who have returned home.

✝ Lord, my heart is not proud, and my eyes are not haughty.

✿ O Lord, I do not occupy myself with matters too great for me.

❖ ¹ I do not occupy myself with things that are too difficult for me.

● I have learned to still my soul and quiet my mind.

❖ ² I quiet my mind like a child upon his mother's breast.

● Like a child my soul is still within me.

❖ ³ From this time forth and forevermore,

● O Israel, put your trust in the Lord.

❖ ⁴ Behold now, bless the Lord, all you servants of the Lord.

● Lift up your hands in the holy place and bless the Lord.

❖ You who stand by night in the house of the Lord, bless the Lord.

✿ May the Lord who made heaven and earth bless you out of Zion.

✝ O Israel, wait upon the Lord, from this time forth forevermore.

Psalm 135

Psalm 135 is a psalm of praise. This is a call to worship aimed at the priests and Levites who are to continue the worship even after the pilgrims have returned home. It recounts numerous reasons why God should be worshiped.

✝ Hallelujah! Praise the name of the LORD; give praise, you servants of the LORD, who stand in the courts of the house of our God.

✿ Praise the LORD, sing praises to God's name, for the LORD is good. For our God has chosen Israel as a precious possession.

❖¹ For I know that the LORD is greater than all other gods. Our God brings forth rain and lightning and winds from the ends of the earth.

● Whatever our LORD pleases will be done on earth and in heaven.

❖² It is God who struck down the firstborn of Egypt, both man and beast, and who sent signs and wonders into the midst of Egypt against Pharaoh and his servants.

● Your everlasting name, O LORD, endures from age to age.

❖³ God overthrew many nations and destroyed mighty kings: Sihon of the Amorites, and Og of Bashan, and the kingdoms of Canaan. Their lands became an inheritance for the people of Israel.

● For the LORD provides justice and compassion to Israel.

❖⁴ The idols of the heathen have mouths but cannot speak, eyes that cannot see, ears that cannot hear; and there is no breath in their mouths.

● Heathen idols of silver and gold are the work of human hands.

❖ Those who make them are like them, and so are all who put their trust in them.

✿ Bless the LORD, O house of Israel, O house of Aaron and house of Levi; you who stand in awe of the LORD, bless the LORD.

✝ Blessed be the LORD out of Zion, who dwells in Jerusalem. Hallelujah!

Psalm 136

This psalm of praise is a call to worship, a call and response in which every verse ends with the same phrase. In this psalm God is extolled as creator, redeemer, guide, champion, and savior.

✝ Give thanks to the LORD, our God of gods, who alone is good. God's loving mercy endures forever.

✪ Give thanks to the LORD of Lords, who alone does marvelous deeds. God's loving mercy endures forever.

❖¹ By wisdom Yahweh made the heavens and spread out the earth over the waters; the LORD created light, the sun to rule the day and the moon and stars to govern the night.

● God's loving mercy endures forever.

❖² The LORD struck down the firstborn of Egypt and brought out Israel from among them, with a mighty hand and a stretched-out arm.

● God's loving mercy endures forever.

❖³ God divided the Red Sea in two so Israel could pass through, but swept Pharaoh and his army into the Red Sea.

● God's loving mercy endures forever.

❖⁴ Yahweh led the Israelites through the wilderness and struck down great kings, Sihon of the Amorites and Og, king of Bashan, and gave away their land for an inheritance.

● God's loving mercy endures forever.

❖ The LORD gave an inheritance to Israel, and this is the same LORD who remembers us in our weakness. God's loving mercy endures forever.

✪ Yahweh rescues us from our enemies and provides food to all creatures. God's loving mercy endures forever.

✝ Give thanks to the LORD of heaven, for God's loving mercy endures forever.

Psalm 137

This national lament recalls the exile into Babylon. Again, this is an imprecatory psalm asking for justice for the destruction done in Israel and especially in Jerusalem. In ancient Israel, it was believed that without children there could be no hope for the future. The last verse of this psalm, then, is not to be taken literally, but as a call for Babylon to be left without hope, for their future to be cut off and utterly destroyed.

✝ By the waters of Babylon we sat down and wept, when we remembered you, O Zion.

✪ On the branches of willow trees we hung up our harps in this strange land.

❖¹ For our captors demanded that we sing a song, and our oppressors called out, saying,

● "Sing to us one of the songs of Zion."

❖² How can we sing the LORD's song in a foreign land?

● Do not let me forget you, O Jerusalem.

❖³ Let my right hand forget its skill and let my tongue stick to the roof of my mouth if I do not remember you, O Jerusalem.

● LORD, help me set Jerusalem as my highest joy.

❖⁴ Remember the day of Jerusalem, O LORD, when the people of Edom declared, "Take it down! Tear it down to its very foundation!"

● Remember your faithful people, O LORD, who were driven out.

❖ O daughter of Babylon, you are doomed for destruction. How blessed is the one who pays you back in kind for all the destruction you have wrought on us!

✪ Happy is he who takes your little ones and dashes them against the rock!

✝ By the waters of Babylon we sat down and wept, when we remembered you, O Zion.

Psalm 138

This individual psalm of thanksgiving is said to be by David. This begins the final set of psalms attributed to David (Psalms 138–145). Here he focuses on God's faithfulness to him personally.

✝   I give you thanks, O LORD, with my whole heart; forever I will sing your praises before the heavenly hosts.

✪   Because of your love and faithfulness, I will bow down toward your holy temple and praise your name.

   ❖¹ For you have glorified your name and exalted your word above all things.

   ● Your word is above all, and your glory shines forth.

   ❖² When I cry out for help, you answer me; you have gladdened my soul by giving me strength.

   ● I will sing of your ways and the glory of the LORD.

   ❖³ All the kings of the earth will give you thanks, O LORD, when they have heard the words of your mouth.

   ● Even kings will sing of your ways, O LORD.

   ❖⁴ The LORD is exalted on high, and yet he cares for the lowly; but the haughty he perceives from afar.

   ● The glory of the LORD will be praised forever.

   ❖ Although I walk in the midst of trouble, you keep me safe.

✪   You stretch forth your hand against the fury of my enemies; for it is your right hand that saves me.

✝   You will fulfill your plan for my life. O LORD, your love endures forever; do not abandon the works of your hands.

Psalm 139, Part 1 (Verses 1–13)

Psalm 139 is a wisdom psalm of David. The intimacy between God and David is seen clearly in this psalm.

✝ Lord, you have searched me out and known me; you know when I sit down and when I rise up again.

✪ You, O Lord, know everything about me; you even discern my thoughts from afar.

❖¹ You know where I journey and where I rest my head; you are acquainted with all my ways.

● O Lord, you know my words even before they form on my lips.

❖² You travel behind me and before me and protect me with your hand. Such wonderful knowledge is beyond my comprehension.

● Such caring is too intense for me to understand.

❖³ Where then can I go from your Spirit? Where can I flee from your presence? If I climb up to heaven, you are there.

● Even in heaven your hand will guide me.

❖⁴ If I make the grave my bed, you are there also. If I take the wings of the morning and dwell on the furthest shores of the sea,

● Even there your right hand will hold me fast.

❖ I could say, "Surely the darkness will cover me, and the light around me will turn to night."

✪ But darkness is not dark to you, O Lord. The night is as bright as the day; darkness and light to you are both alike.

✝ For you yourself created my inmost parts; you knit me together in my mother's womb.

Psalm 139, Part 2 (Verses 13–24)

This wisdom psalm of David shows clearly the intimacy between God and David.

✝ You, O LORD, created my inmost parts; you knit me together in my mother's womb.

✿ I give thanks to you, O LORD, because I am marvelously made; your works are awesome, and I know it well.

❖¹ My body was not hidden from you while I was being made in secret and woven in the depths of the earth.

● Your eyes beheld my form, yet unfinished in the womb.

❖² All the days of my life were ordained and planned; they were written in your book even before I drew my first breath.

● How precious I find your thoughts, O God!

❖³ How great is the sum of your thoughts, O God! If counted, they would be more than the grains of sand. When I awaken, O LORD, you are still with me.

● How marvelous are your many thoughts, O God!

❖⁴ Oh, if only you would slay the wicked, O God, and remove the bloodthirsty ones from my presence! They speak maliciously about you, and they take your name in vain.

● Search me, O LORD, and know my heart.

❖ I despise those who hate you, O LORD, and loathe those who rise up against you. I count them all as my enemies.

✿ Search me out, O God, and know my heart; try me and know my restless thoughts.

✝ Seek out any wickedness in me, O LORD, and lead me in the path of everlasting life.

Psalm 140

This psalm is an individual lament by David. David's faith in Yahweh remains firm even in the face of deceitful enemies.

✝ Deliver me, O LORD, from evildoers; protect me from violent enemies.

☉ Protect me from those who devise evil in their hearts and stir up conflict all day long.

❖¹ They have sharpened their tongues like a serpent's; viper's poison flows from their lips. Protect me from the wicked who are determined to trip me up.

● Keep me safe, O LORD, from the hands of the wicked.

❖² The arrogant have hidden a snare for me and stretched out a net of cords along my path. I have cried out to the LORD,

● "You are my God! Listen, O LORD, to my plea for mercy."

❖³ O LORD God, the strength of my salvation, you have shielded my head in the day of battle. Do not grant the desires of the wicked.

● O LORD, do not let their evil plans succeed.

❖⁴ As for those who surround me, may they be overwhelmed by their own lies. Let burning coals fall upon them.

● O LORD, come to my rescue and render justice.

❖ Let them be cast into the miry pits, never to rise up again. Let no slanderer prosper on the earth, but let disaster fall on those who are evil.

☉ I know that the LORD will defend the cause of the poor and render justice to the oppressed.

✝ Surely the righteous will give thanks to your name, and the upright will dwell in your presence.

Psalm 141

Psalm 141 is an individual lament attributed to David. David's desire to live with integrity is seen here as he requests God's help in resisting temptations laid out by his enemies.

✝ O LORD, come to me quickly and hear my voice when I cry out to you.

✪ Let my prayer be set forth in your sight as incense, and may the lifting up of my hands be as the evening sacrifice.

❖¹ Set a guard over my mouth, O LORD, and watch over the door of my lips.

● Do not let my heart be drawn to evil desires.

❖² Let me not participate in sinful activities with evildoers, nor eat of their delicacies.

● Let only the righteous correct me in friendly rebuke.

❖³ The reproof of a godly person is like oil upon my head. Yet my prayer is continually against the wicked deeds of evildoers. Let their rulers be thrown from a cliff.

● Let them understand that my words are true.

❖⁴ As when a plowman reveals stones in the overturned earth, let their bones be scattered at the entrance of Sheol.

● My eyes are turned to you, LORD God; you are my refuge.

❖ I take refuge in you, Yahweh, my LORD; do not leave me defenseless.

✪ Protect me from the snare that they have laid for me and from the traps set by evildoers. Let the wicked fall into their own nets, while I myself escape to safety.

✝ O LORD, come to me quickly and hear my voice when I cry out to you.

Psalm 142

Psalm 142 is an individual lament by David, a *maskil* about the time he hid in a cave from Saul. Much of the psalm is in third person, which is not uncommon when speaking to royalty.

✝ I cry aloud to the LORD with my voice; to the LORD I make my fervent plea.

✪ I pour out my complaint before him and tell him all my trouble.

❖¹ Even when my spirit languishes within me, you know the way I travel; they have hidden a trap for me in the path where I walk.

● O LORD, watch over my steps as I travel.

❖² I look to my right, but I can find no one to help. There is no place to escape and no one who cares about me.

● I cry to you in my distress; O LORD, help me.

❖³ I cry out to you, O LORD, and say, "You are my refuge, my portion in the land of the living.

● Hear my cry, O loving God of my salvation."

❖⁴ Listen to my cry for help, for I am in desperate need. Save me from my persecutors, for they are too strong for me.

● Come quickly to my rescue, O LORD.

❖ Bring me out of my prison, so I may give thanks to your name.

✪ When you have dealt bountifully with me, the righteous will gather around me.

✝ I cry aloud to the LORD with my voice; to the LORD I make my fervent plea.

Psalm 143

In this individual lament, David cries out to God for help. He relied not on his own obedience to God but on the very nature of God's faithfulness to rescue his beloved children.

✝ Hear my prayer, O LORD, and in your faithfulness listen to my supplication; answer me in your righteousness.

✤ Do not sit in judgment on your servant, for in your sight no living person could be justified.

❖¹ For my enemies have sought my life and crushed me to the ground. They have made me live in dark places like those who are long dead.

● My spirit is overwhelmed, and my heart is dismayed.

❖² I remember days of old; I meditate on all your deeds and ponder the works of your hands. I stretch out my hands to you.

● My soul longs for you like parched land thirsts for rain.

❖³ O LORD, hasten to answer me, for my spirit fails me. Do not hide your face from me, or I will be like one going down to the Pit.

● Let the morning bring me word of your loving kindness.

❖⁴ I put my trust in you, O LORD. Show me the road that I must travel, for I lift up my soul to you. Deliver me from my enemies.

● Deliver me when I take refuge in you, O LORD.

❖ Teach me to do your will, for you are my God. Let your gracious Spirit lead me to level ground.

✤ Revive me, O LORD, for your name's sake; and in your righteousness, deliver my soul from trouble.

✝ In your goodness, O LORD, silence my enemies and destroy all my foes, for truly I am your servant.

Psalm 144

Psalm 144 is a royal psalm of David, probably written after he became established as king over the united tribes of Judah and Israel.

✝ Blessed be the LORD, my rock, who trains my hands to fight and my fingers for battle. You, LORD, are my loving God.

✪ You are my fortress, my stronghold, and my deliverer, my shield in whom I trust. You subdue the nations under me.

❖¹ O LORD, what are we, mere mortals, that you should care for us? We are like a breath of wind; our days are like a passing shadow.

● Bend down from heaven, O LORD, to touch the mountains.

❖² Hurl the lightning and scatter my enemies; shoot your arrows to rout them. Stretch out your hand to rescue me from great waters.

● Deliver me from the hand of hostile enemies.

❖³ They tell lies, and they vow false promises. O God, I will sing to you a new song and play on a ten-stringed lyre.

● For you give victory to kings, and you rescued David from the sword.

❖⁴ Deliver me, O LORD, from the hand of foreign powers, whose mouths speak deceitfully and whose right hand is raised in a lie.

● May our sons in their youth grow quickly to full stature.

❖ And may our daughters be like the graceful pillars of a palace. May our barns be overflowing with all varieties of crops and our cattle bear heavy loads.

✪ May the flocks in our pastures increase by tens of thousands. There will be no breaching of the walls, no going into exile, and no wailing in the public square.

✝ Blessed are the people of whom this is true! Blessed are the people whose God is Yahweh!

Psalm 145

This psalm of praise attributed to David is an acrostic poem with verses beginning with successive letters of the Hebrew alphabet.

✝ I will exalt you, O God my King. Every day I will bless you and praise your name forever and ever.

☯ Great is the LORD and worthy of praise. Each generation shall praise your works and declare your unending greatness.

❖¹ Others speak of your mighty acts, but I will ponder the glorious splendor of your majesty and tell of your marvelous works. They publish the remembrance of your great goodness.

● They eagerly sing praises of your righteousness.

❖² The LORD is gracious and merciful, slow to anger and full of great kindness. All your works praise you, O LORD; your followers bless you.

● The LORD is loving and full of compassion for all.

❖³ Your followers speak of your glory and might, so their children may know of your power and the majestic splendor of your kingdom.

● Your kingdom, O LORD, is an everlasting kingdom.

❖⁴ Your dominion endures through all ages. O LORD, you are faithful in your words and merciful deeds. You love all you have made. You lift up those who fall and who are bowed down.

● All things look to you, O LORD, for you give them food in due season.

❖ You open your hand to satisfy the needs of every living creature. You, O LORD, are righteous in all your ways and loving to all that you made.

✿ You, O Lord, are near to all who call upon you faithfully. You fulfill the desires of those who revere you; you hear their cries and come to their aid.

✝ O Lord, you protect all who love you, but you destroy the wicked. My mouth will sing praises to the Lord. Let every creature bless your holy name forever and ever.

Psalm 146

Psalm 146 is a psalm of praise. The five final psalms all begin and end with "Hallelujah!" Here we are reminded of the multiple ways in which God shows his loving kindness.

✝ Hallelujah! Praise the LORD, O my soul! I will praise the LORD as long as I live. I will sing praises to my God while I have my being.

☉ Put not your trust in rulers nor in any child of earth, for there is no help in them.

❖¹ When they breathe their last, they return to earth, and in that day their thoughts perish.

● Happy are they who have the God of Jacob for their help!

❖² The God of Jacob made heaven and earth, the seas, and all that is in them; the LORD remains faithful forever.

● Happy are they whose hope is in the LORD their God.

❖³ The LORD God gives justice to those who are oppressed and food to those who hunger.

● The LORD lifts up those who are bowed down.

❖⁴ The LORD sets the prisoners free and opens the eyes of the blind.

● The LORD loves the righteous and cares for the stranger.

❖ Our God loves the righteous; God protects the stranger and sustains the orphan and widow.

☉ But our God will frustrate the plans of the wicked.

✝ The LORD shall reign forever, your God, O Zion, throughout all generations. Hallelujah!

Psalm 147

This psalm of praise may have been written to celebrate the restoration of Jerusalem after the Babylonian exile.

✝ Hallelujah! How good it is to sing praises to our God! How pleasant it is to honor God with a song of praise!

○ The LORD rebuilds Jerusalem and gathers the exiles of Israel. God will heal the brokenhearted and bind up their wounds. Our LORD counts the number of the stars and calls them each by name.

❖¹ The LORD lifts up the humble but casts down the wicked. Sing to the LORD with thanksgiving; make music to our God upon the harp.

● Great is our LORD, mighty in power, with unlimited wisdom.

❖² Our LORD covers the heavens with clouds, prepares rain for the earth, and makes grass to grow upon the hills.

● You provide food for herds and ravens when they cry out.

❖³ Our LORD is not impressed by the might of a horse or the legs of a man, but God takes pleasure in those who revere and await God's gracious favor.

● Worship the LORD, O Jerusalem; praise your God, O Zion.

❖⁴ For God has strengthened the bars of your gates and blessed your children within you. The LORD has established peace on your borders and satisfies you with the finest wheat.

● Your words fly swiftly to deliver your command to the earth.

❖ The LORD gives snow like wool and scatters frost like ashes. God scatters hail like breadcrumbs; who can withstand this cold?

○ God's word melts them all, and then the wind blows and the waters begin to flow. O LORD, you declare your word to Jacob, your statutes and judgments to Israel.

✝ God has not done so to any other nation; they do not know of God's righteous judgments. Hallelujah!

Psalm 148

Psalm 148 is a psalm of praise. Everything in heaven and on earth joins together to sing praise to the LORD.

✝ Hallelujah! Praise the LORD from the heavens; praise God in the heights.

✪ Praise God, all you angels and all the heavenly host. Praise God, sun and moon and all you shining stars.

❖¹ Praise God, you highest heavens, and you waters above the heavens. Let them praise the name of the LORD.

● At God's command the heavens and all therein were created.

❖² God established them forever and gave them a decree that will not pass away. Even the sea monsters and everything in the ocean depths,

● All these will praise the LORD God of heaven and earth.

❖³ Fire and hail, snow and fog, tempestuous wind are doing God's will, mountains and all hills, fruit trees and all cedars.

● The earth and all therein, praise the name of the LORD.

❖⁴ Wild beasts and cattle of the field, small scurrying animals and birds of the air,

● Let all creatures praise the name of the LORD.

❖ Kings of the earth and all peoples, princes and all rulers of the world, praise the name of the LORD.

✪ Young men and maidens, old and young together, let them praise the name of the LORD, for God's name only is exalted, and the splendor of the LORD covers all of heaven and earth.

✝ O LORD, you raised up strength and praise for all your faithful people, the children of Israel, a people who are near to their God. Hallelujah!

Psalm 149

This psalm of praise encourages singing a new song to God, praising him for past and recent blessings.

† Hallelujah! Sing to the LORD a new song; sing God's praise in the congregation of the faithful.

☉ Let Israel rejoice in their Maker; let the children of Zion be joyful in their King.

❖¹ Let them praise God's name in the dance; let them sing praises with timbrel and harp.

● Let us sing praises to the LORD our God.

❖² For the LORD takes pleasure in the faithful and brings beauty to the humble through salvation.

● Our LORD God has done great things for us.

❖³ Let the faithful exult in glory and sing for joy on their beds at night.

● All the faithful rejoice in the LORD their God.

❖⁴ Let the praises of God be in their throat and a double-edged sword in their hand.

● The LORD has empowered the faithful here on earth,

❖ To execute vengeance on the nations and punishment on the peoples,

☉ To bind up their kings in chains and their nobles with iron shackles,

† To inflict on enemies the judgment decreed. This is the glory of all God's faithful people. Hallelujah!

Psalm 150

Psalm 150, the final psalm in the book of Psalms, is a psalm of corporate praise. It is an appeal for all creation to find its true destiny and identity through the worship of God.

† Hallelujah! Praise God in the sanctuary.

☉ Hallelujah! Praise God in the mighty heavens.

❖¹ Praise God for the mighty acts of power and for abundant greatness.

● We praise you, O LORD, for your excellent greatness.

❖² Praise God with the blast of the ram's horn and with the lyre and harp.

● We praise you, O LORD, with instruments of glorious music.

❖³ Praise God with timbrel and dance; praise God with strings and flute.

● We praise you, O LORD, with both song and dance.

❖⁴ Praise God with loud cymbals, with loud-clanging cymbals.

● We praise you, O LORD, with resounding cymbals.

❖ Let everything that has breath praise the LORD.

☉ Praise God in the sanctuary, God's holy temple in the firmament of heaven.

† Let everything that has breath praise the LORD our God. Hallelujah!

Additional Resources for the Anglican Rosary

Rosaries

Rosaries may be ordered from the Solitaries of Dekoven at this web address: http://solitariesofdekoven.org/store/.

They may also be ordered from Full Circle Beads at https://full circlebeads.com.

Books

Doerr, Nan Lewis, and Virginia Stem Owens. *Praying with Beads: Daily Prayers for the Christian Year.* Grand Rapids: Eerdmans, 2007.

Elliott, Kristin M., and Betty Kay Seibt. *Holding Your Prayers in Your Hands.* Available from Open Hands, 624 West University Drive, Suite 110, Denton, TX 76201.

Elliott, Kristin M., and Betty Kay Seibt. *Praying the Way of the Cross with the Anglican Rosary.* Available from Open Hands, 624 West University Drive, Suite 110, Denton, TX 76201.

Hamilton, Cindy. *Praying through the Psalms: A Guide for Contemplative Prayer Using Anglican Prayer Beads.* Available from Pembroke Street Press, 307 South State Street, Nampa, ID 83686.

Vincent, Kristen E. *A Bead and a Prayer: A Beginner's Guide to Protestant Prayer Beads.* Nashville: Upper Room Books, 2013.